TRAVELS WITH MY OPERA GLASSES

A Fanatic's Tales of Delights and Disappointments

ANTHONY OGUS

Foreword by SIR THOMAS ALLEN

Published by

MELROSE
BOOKS

An Imprint of Melrose Press Limited
St Thomas Place, Ely
Cambridgeshire
CB7 4GG, UK
www.melrosebooks.co.uk

FIRST EDITION

Cover designed by Lynne McPeake

ISBN 978-1-908645-53-1

Printed and bound in Great Britain by:
Mimeo Ltd, Huntingdon, Cambridgeshire

FSC
www.fsc.org
MIX
From responsible
sources
FSC® C019549

TABLE OF CONTENTS

*To Michael, who made so much of this possible
and who produced a son whose enthusiasm for opera
restored my faith in the younger generation.*

FOREWORD

In the months surrounding the bicentenary of Mozart's death in 1991, like many singers, I found myself travelling the world—Figaro chasing Count chasing Don Giovanni—night after night after night. I even wrote about the period in a book that formed a journal of a hectic eighteen-month period of my working life. Readers remarked on their breathlessness in following me as I chased around the globe.

I took delight in pooh-poohing the idea that any of it was a trouble to me. But now, twenty years later, reading Anthony's book of his exploits from the other side of the velvet curtain, I am the one left breathless and astounded. In fact I'm always astounded when I encounter the passion of opera lovers around the world. The book is a compendium of operatic delights recounted by a true connoisseur.

What I really like about Anthony's passion is that he is not led by fashion and hyperbole as to what is IN, but is always the man with his own mind. He is able to single out the less glamorous places, the less-than-ritzy performances—of Fidelio, for example—that go to the core of one's being, strike the heart. Only the real connoisseur recognises those special moments.

The book makes a most enlightening read, and will appeal to those enjoying opera on EVERY level.

ACKNOWLEDGMENTS

I should like to express my gratitude: to Sir Thomas Allen for his lively and friendly Foreword; to Lynne McPeake for her superb cover; to Sue Bate, Caroline Bridge, Gerbert Faure, Christopher Hodges and John Trotman for most helpful comments and advice; to Nicholas Payne who found time in between many more important activities to spot and correct a number of errors; to the staff at Melrose Books who displayed a confidence in the product not entirely shared by other publishers; and most of all to Helen Owens who, apart from giving me help in describing the dress of opera audiences, sustained my more general efforts with her enthusiasm and encouragement.

CHAPTER ONE

INTRODUCTION: OPERAMANIA

It was May 1962. Aged then sixteen, I had been slow to appreciate classical music, but was keen on theatre. I thought it was time to give opera a try, never having been to it before. I lived in a London suburb, so the Royal Opera Covent Garden was the obvious place to start. But what should I see? There was no one in the family, or a friend, who was an opera-goer and who could advise me. The red and yellow posters at my local station told me that, during the weeks ahead, performances would be given of *Madama Butterfly*, *La Bohème*, *Aida*, and *A Midsummer Night's Dream*.

Now, you might have expected me to opt for *Aida*, which had the great Russian soprano Galina Vishnevskaya in the title role, or *La Bohème*, which even I, in my ignorant state, was aware was a popular work, and this revival boasted Victoria de los Angeles among its cast. But no, I chose Britten's *Dream*, primarily because I knew and loved the play, and therefore thought that it would be a good starting point. I was wrong: Britten's airy-fairy music did not appeal, and I was unsettled by the sound of a counter-tenor voice, which was used for the leading role of Oberon but which was completely new to me. The work was later to become one of my favourite twentieth-century operas, capturing as it does so well the spirit and also the language of Shakespeare, but it was not a sensible choice for my initiation.

It was a year or so before my next operatic outing, and even then I studiously avoided the popular Italian repertory, perhaps because, with the arrogance of an aspiring intellectual sixth-former, I suspected that it was insufficiently highbrow. But, once I had gratified my snobbism with Stravinsky's *Rake's Progress* and the Brecht/Weill piece *The Rise and Fall of the City of Mahagonny*, both admirably staged at Sadlers Wells, I was soon into Mozart, Wagner, and yes, at last, Verdi and Puccini. In 1965, a holiday in Italy which included performances of *Rigoletto*, *Aida* and *Turandot* finally cured me of my absurd prejudices and I was now truly hooked on opera.

During my student days, I explored most of the mainstream repertory. I listened to recordings of some of the pieces at home, thanks to the invaluable local record library. Some I came to know through piano-accompanied concert performances given by the Oxford University Opera Club at the Holywell Music Rooms. I also made regular visits to Covent Garden and Sadlers Wells though, because my budget was limited, invariably in the cheaper seats or standing at the back of the Stalls Circle.

Obtaining employment as a university lecturer, and the purchase of my first car, enabled me to extend geographically the range of my operatic experiences; and that included the festival scene. During August 1967, I drove my Mini through the Alps to Verona where I attended two performances at the famous Arena—in those days, you simply turned up and paid 2000 lire for a ticket. Back across the Brenner Pass to the Munich Festival, and then, the climax of the trip, to Bayreuth. Wagner was then my favourite composer, and in a period of eight days I saw six of his works: *Rienzi* and *Meistersinger* at Munich, and the four evenings of the *Ring* in Bayreuth.

Yes, it can truly be said that I had succumbed to operamania, and the disease was at its most ravaging during the 1970s. One highlight was a tour of Czechoslovakia which included experiences both operatic and political—this was the period of the clampdown after the Prague Spring. Both experiences proved to be memorable and moving, and I wrote an account of them which was published in the Berlin opera magazine *Orpheus*. This led to an invitation to become the journal's British correspondent, and for eighteen glorious months I had free tickets for performances at Covent Garden and elsewhere.

It made me feel very grand to pop into the press office, chat to the press officer, and survey the production photographs. I also enjoyed composing the reviews, but there was a problem. My German was not good enough to write the final version myself, and so I had to find someone to help me with the language. In the end, that proved to be too difficult to arrange and, for that and other reasons, in 1977 I had to resign. Perhaps it was just as well, because in the following year I was appointed to a Chair at the University of Newcastle upon Tyne and this city, fine though it is, was not very convenient for travelling to the most important British opera performances.

I have lived in the North of England ever since. Let me say at once that this is far from being an operatic wilderness. The regional company, Opera North, has its base in Leeds and, under the inspired leadership of Richard Mantle, has been remarkable both for its enterprise and for the quality of its performances. Then there is the Royal Northern College of Music at Manchester, which has been responsible for the training of many of Britain's top singers. Of course, Covent Garden and the Coliseum were less frequently on my agenda. Nevertheless, as my academic career developed, so did the number of invitations for visits to universities abroad. And, as my foreign colleagues soon began to appreciate, my willingness to accept such invitations became much the keener if I could combine my professional obligations with operatic performances in the vicinity. And so it continued until my retirement in 2011.

In May 2012, I celebrated fifty years of operamania. If you still need convincing that this is an appropriate word to use, let me bore you with some statistics. By December 2012 I had attended 1346 operatic performances: 684 of these had been abroad (in 24 countries); 662 in the

3

UK. I prefer not to estimate how much I have spent on tickets because that would be too embarrassing. The 1340 outings have involved 575 different operas, but if you think that would include all those featured in the latest edition of Kobbé's *Complete Opera Book*, you would be wrong. Of the 310 there, I have 41 still to go. So, if you have information where I might find a performance of, for example, *The Immortal Hour* by Roland Boughton, or *Le Postillon de Longjumeau* by Adolphe Adam, please let me know. Of the more familiar entries, those which I have seen most frequently are mainly by Mozart: I have been to 19 performances of both *Die Zauberflöte* and *Don Giovanni*, one more than *Le Nozze di Figaro*. But Wagner's *Das Rheingold* has also notched up 19. The Verdi operas, which have scored best with 13, are *Don Carlos* and—somewhat to my surprise—*La Traviata*.

Operamania is not, however, about statistics; it is about a state of mind. It reveals itself when I pore through my copy of the monthly *Opera* magazine, when I plan my next "excursion", when I have an "opera gossip" with other fanatics; but, most of all, when I am in the theatre and the lights go down, I get this *frisson*. Admittedly, as will become clear in Chapter Four, on occasions this will be caused by apprehension that someone will emerge from behind the curtain to announce that, for one reason or other, the performance is cancelled. But, more often, it will be eager anticipation of the pleasures to come.

What is it, then, that gives so much pleasure? Obviously, it is the combination of music and drama. I enjoy both of these when taken separately, but put them together and the result is irresistible. It can occur, for example, in a solo aria expressing a character's emotions, a duet or ensemble entwining the different thoughts of different individuals, or simply the orchestra giving its own aural version of what is happening on stage. If you were to ask me which is more important, the music or the drama—a debate which features in operas by Salieri (*Primo la musica e poi le parole*)) and Richard Strauss (*Capriccio*)—I would be unable to answer. They are completely symbiotic. Wonderful singing or a great conductor can transcend the limitations of a mediocre libretto or a misguided production, but equally a strong dramatic content or a powerful production can make one more tolerant of a musically disappointing performance.

It follows that I am not to be categorised among the "canary fanciers", those who go to opera mainly to hear great singers show off their vocal talents. To turn up to the umpteenth revival of *Tosca* to find out how the latest *diva* from Armenia, or wherever, compares with her predecessors has never seemed to me to be particularly worthwhile. Indeed, I tend to avoid performances at the big international houses when star singers are flown in to perform in stale old productions. However gifted these stars may be, such an occasion typically does not generate great musical theatre—that requires imaginative staging and a well-integrated ensemble effort.

It is also valuable to have variety in what you see, and where you see it. In my operatic outings, I like to maintain a balance between the major opera houses, regional companies, and what may be described as "fringe" performances, those given by students or by small touring groups, working with very modest resources. Each of these will have a different type of audience and a different atmosphere.

It is of course always impressive to enter the hallowed halls of the Vienna Staatsoper or La Scala and to feel the heritage of the place as well as its architecture. If you are lucky you may even hit upon a performance worthy of its history. But I do not exaggerate when I claim that attending a performance at, say, the Royal Northern College of Music can be just as exciting an operatic experience even though, in terms simply of musical standards, the quality will (or should) be higher at the famous venue. When aspiring young singers throw themselves with energy and commitment into a performance, this creates an atmosphere which enhances the impact of the music and drama. Add to this the enthusiasm with which the audience at this kind of event usually responds, partly, no doubt, because it contains many friends and family of the students, and you can have a very good evening. It was, incidentally, at the RNCM in 2004 that I celebrated, with a champagne party, my one thousandth operatic outing—a typically exciting performance of *The Rake's Progress*.

More generally, as I will show in Chapter Six, the character, behaviour and dress of audiences vary between countries and also between venues within countries. One of the opera fanatic's real pleasures is to observe and mingle with, on the one hand, the Glyndebourne set and, on the other, those attending a small-scale performance in, say, Skipton, and who may be real enthusiasts enjoying a rare opportunity to have opera on their doorstep or simply newcomers to the noble art, curious to find out what it is all about.

As regards excursions abroad, it is intriguing to get away from the major operatic centres, Milan, Paris, Berlin, and experience the offerings at smaller theatres in less familiar locations, such as Lucca, Massy, or Altenburg. To your surprise, you may find there a strong tradition, going back to the nineteenth century, with perhaps a loyal, local following, or else a company which has a reputation for innovative or imaginative performances.

Then there are the questions of range of works and artistic goals. Routine is the antithesis of opera at its best, and it can too easily creep in because many companies will be wary of straying far from works which are familiar and which make for good business in terms of box-office receipts. There is a core repertory of about thirty operas which regularly reappear in the programmes of most companies (*Figaro*, *Rigoletto*, *Carmen*, *Tosca* and so on). Such pieces must surely lose their allure if seen too often when performed in the same way (that ballet audiences should be prepared to return time and again to similar versions of *Swan Lake* and *The Nutcracker* has always seemed very odd to me).

Beyond the core, there are 100 or so works which the average opera-goer might have a good chance of seeing without travelling too far. But I confess that, as the years have gone by, I have derived more and more pleasure from seeking out rarities. I might not be a "canary fancier", but I own up to being the opera-going equivalent of a bird-loving "twitcher", someone who will journey far to see a rare species. In November 2011, for example, I proudly added to my list *L'Africaine* by Meyerbeer, which I saw in Würzburg and, four days later, Weinberger's *Schwanda the Bagpiper* in Görlitz.

It has to be said that some neglected works have turned out to be neglected for very good reasons. No doubt the artistic director of the Buxton Festival thought that anything by Franz Schubert was worth an airing, but when *Fierrabras* was given there in 2000, the performance left me amazed as to how the composer of such sophisticated musical-dramatic masterpieces as the song cycle *Die Winterreise* could have written such embarrassing, naïve tosh about love and chivalric honour. But others have been delightful discoveries: *The Taming of the Shrew* by Hermann Goetz; *Le Roi Arthus* by Ernest Chausson; and *A Dinner Engagement* by Lennox Berkeley, to name but a few.

You do not have to go to a theatre to experience opera. It can be performed in a concert hall, either in a semi-staged version—the singers, appropriately costumed and without scores move and interact with each other, and there may be some props and lighting effects—or else in pure concert form, as though it were an oratorio. You can hear it at home on a CD or broadcast on the radio. You can watch a DVD, either of a film of the opera or of a recording of a stage production. These days you can also go to a cinema and see there a live transmission of a performance.

The concert version may have been chosen because a fully staged version would, in the locality, have been too difficult or, as can be the case with Wagner, too expensive to mount. Or it may be thought that the work in question is unlikely to attract audiences in sufficient numbers to justify a theatrical staging which would run for several performances. There is a splendid organisation, the Chelsea Opera Group, which, for many years, has specialised in this form of presentation. Indeed, one of the highlights of my early opera-going was *Les Troyens à Carthage* by Berlioz given in 1964 by this group at the Oxford Town Hall, conducted by Colin Davis and with a young Josephine Veasey in the role of Dido.

Now you might think that the response of an operamaniac to a concert version would be that of frustration, particularly if it is one where, say, Alberich the power-mad dwarf in *Das Rheingold* barks out his curse on the Ring wearing a bow tie and tails, and singing from a score; and you would be right. On the other hand, there are some important compensations. Cost is one of them, since ticket prices should be reasonable compared with what you have to fork out for seats at most opera houses. Then, not having the distraction of stage business can also enable you—and the singers!—to concentrate on the music. You can also use your imagination to create for yourself images to match the music and, given some of the horrors that are perpetrated on us by contemporary stage directors, you may even be better off in the concert hall.

Live transmissions, particularly from the New York Met and Covent Garden, have become very popular in recent years. Being suspicious of the phenomenon, I ventured to it for the first time only in 2012. In many ways I was impressed. The sound quality was very good and you had a better view of what was happening on stage than you would have had from almost any seat in a theatre. For about twenty per cent of the cost of an average-priced ticket at one of the world's great opera houses, you could see and hear the top singers of the day, and without travelling further than to your local cinema. This is surely a boon for the many who cannot get to, or who cannot afford the prices of, "real" performances at opera houses. It also must serve to whet the appetite of those for whom opera is a new experience.

At the same time, some of my forebodings were confirmed. I missed the physicality of the performers in the theatre, communicating—or so it seems—to me personally. I missed the sense of space and depth of the stage presentation, partly because I was only too well aware of the flat cinema screen, but also because most of the relay consisted of close-ups of those singing, whether soloists or chorus. Now, since my days up in the "gods" at Covent Garden, I have regularly taken opera glasses to performances—during my fifty years of opera-going I have lost only one pair, and this has been something of an achievement, given the number of umbrellas, scarves and caps which I have left in various places. But I use the glasses only spasmodically, when it is important for me that I have a close-up view of a particular singer. At the transmission, the choice of what I was looking at was not mine, but that of the broadcasting director and I did not always share his or her view of what was important. By way of analogy, when I am at a football or rugby match, I sometimes prefer to see what players are doing "off the ball" and this applies also to opera. So, until I reach my dotage, I shall be sticking to opera mainly in the theatre.

In 1981 a group called Pavilion Opera was launched, and it began to specialise in touring stately homes with piano-accompanied performances that could be fitted into dining rooms, libraries and so on. I saw their production of Donizetti's comic opera, *L'Elisir d'Amore* at Chesters, a fine Northumberland mansion adjacent to Hadrian's Wall and only a stone's throw from where I then lived. Those who purchased tickets were treated to a glass of wine before the performance, and another during the interval. My impression was that the audience was largely made up of the local landed gentry, and was probably more familiar with hunt balls than opera. The performance was given in Italian and, because those present could understand little of the text, the cast had to communicate the comedy through visual gags. The result was a silly, vulgar show which did not do justice to Donizetti's witty piece.

Why was an English translation not used? All the singers were British. Was this an example of artistic authenticity, the Pavilion Opera purists concerned that the blending of music and the sound of the Italian language in the original should not be lost? I doubt it. It seemed to me that it was rather a case of reinforcing the stereotyped image which some social groups might have had of opera as an exotic, elitist *divertissement*.

That experience in Northumberland epitomised for me what was the least attractive side to the way opera might be performed in the "old days". Little of that now goes on because opera-going has become less of an elitist activity. A greater range of people seem to want to experience it, even though it is a costly form of pleasure. You sometimes even see young people at performances, in notable contrast to classical music concerts where the audiences appear to have become increasingly geriatric.

Looking back on the Northumberland episode, I am convinced that one important factor in the wider appreciation of opera was the advent of surtitles in the late 1980s. You cannot fully appreciate the drama if you have only a vague sense of what is being sung. Most performances, then and now, are sung in the original language and, when they began to be accompanied by the projection of a translation of the text, overnight this revolutionised the accessibility of opera. Even when the performance is given in the audience's own language, the text is often difficult to follow, because the voice is covered by the orchestral sound or the singers' articulation is insufficiently clear. And—as we shall see in Chapter Six—surtitles are now often provided in this situation as well. The result has been a much closer involvement of the audience in what is going on and in consequence a more enjoyable experience of musical drama.

Now, if technology has come to the aid of singers who are not good at articulating the text, what about those who have insufficient vocal power? It is commonplace for voices to be amplified in staged musicals, the singers wearing little microphones somewhere around their head, so why not in operas? As far as I know, no conventional opera house has gone down this road, though amplification by this means is sometimes used when opera is given in large, particularly open-air, arenas. Presumably this accords with what the majority of opera-goers want, a preference for hearing the "natural" voice, even though, in some circumstances, it might make a disappointingly small sound.

So the purists have had their way—or have they? In recent years, some theatres, including the New York City Opera and the Staatsoper in Berlin have installed systems of so-called acoustic enhancement. These involve microphones placed strategically around the stage and connected to a discreet series of loudspeakers in the auditorium. The ostensible justification has been that, in some theatres, there are acoustic "dead spots" in parts of the house, and the system, which is coordinated through computers, produces an even distribution of sound. But what may serve this admittedly desirable goal may also, if the operators are so inclined, be used to fortify vocal production, and the line between correcting the acoustic deficiencies of the theatre and boosting the singers' voices becomes a thin one.

We should also recognise that the distance between opera and other forms of theatre, most obviously the musical, is not that large and that fact may have contributed to the increased popularity of opera. Once opera is disassociated from its erstwhile elitist image, some of the many who flock to see *Oliver* and *Oklahoma* might enjoy *Porgy and Bess* or *The Threepenny Opera*, and beyond that *Carmen* and *La Bohème*.

Nor should we forget the "Three Tenors" phenomenon. It started off with Luciano Pavarotti, who recorded *Nessun dorma*, the famous aria from *Turandot*, as the television theme song for the football World Cup held in Italy in 1990. Within weeks this reached number two in the UK singles chart. On the eve of the final, Pavarotti was joined by José Carreras and Placido Domingo in a concert at the Caracalla Baths in Rome. Originally designed to raise money for the Carreras Leukaemia Foundation—the singer had recently recovered from the disease—the concept took off commercially, and concerts in other locations, as well as recordings, ensued. The sound of the full-throated Italianate tenor voice is, of course, thrilling and was doubtless the main reason for the success of the venture. But it also brought operatic music to the attention of a much wider public, and many who had come to realise that it contained some very good tunes must have been tempted to try out the "real thing" in the theatre.

There have been other developments in the opera world since the early 1960s. Perhaps the most striking has been the addition of baroque opera to the repertory. There used to be occasional outings of works by, for example, Monteverdi, Rameau and Handel, but they were performed largely by specialists and attracted only small and rather select audiences who were "into" early music. The breakthrough occurred when conductors such as Raymond Leppard and Charles Mackerras were able to convince a broader-based public of the musical merits of works from this period. But there was still the problem of finding a viable style for the theatrical presentation, stage directors having not devised good methods of dealing with the "stop-start" character of the drama, and the often long solo arias. Eventually this too was overcome as it was realised that with economy of stage movements and imaginative visual settings the drama could be communicated effectively.

At the other end of the time spectrum, Janáček's wonderful operas are now regularly performed, and some of Britten's pieces have entered the repertory, but there are still significant obstacles to the presentation of modern works. The most important of these is money. It is very expensive to mount a full-scale production which is likely to be given only a handful of performances and for which the public response is at best uncertain. Understandably, therefore, contemporary composers have been encouraged to write chamber operas for a small number of soloists, a reduced orchestra and no chorus. From this stable have emerged some powerful works which have proved to have staying power, in the sense that they have enjoyed a number of revivals after their early performances. *The Lighthouse* by Peter Maxwell Davies and *Greek* by Mark-Anthony Turnage are two prominent examples.

So, is the early twenty-first century a good time for operamania? I would respond with a resounding "Yes", though there are negative aspects which must be weighed up against the positive. The recent flourishing of opera has been made possible by public subsidy. Now while the level of such support in Britain has been small compared with that of our continental neighbours, it has not been trivial. In the present economic climate, substantial cuts must be envisaged and some are already beginning to take effect. At the time of writing this, Opera North has had to postpone two new productions which were planned for the end of 2011–12 season.

Private sponsorship may help to deal with the deficit, but this is always easier to raise for the higher-profiled opera companies in London than for those in the provinces. Also, while, as we have seen, large numbers are now attending live transmissions of operas in local cinemas, and this must boost the income of the companies from whom the relay is taken, hitherto the relays have been confined to international, starry performances at Covent Garden, the Met and elsewhere.

Financial support is also a cause for concern abroad, even though the starting point from which cuts are to be made is, in most European countries, significantly higher than in the UK. For example, in 2011, the Dutch government announced a sixty percent reduction in the grant made to the touring company Reisopera. And in Italy, the historical home of opera, the future of performances outside the major centres—Milan, Rome, Naples, Turin, Venice and Bologna—is appearing increasingly uncertain.

What about the quality of performances? Have standards gone up, or were things better in the "good old days"? Well, orchestral playing in the pit has certainly improved and so have the singing and acting of the chorus on the stage. As regards soloists, there may be fewer really great stars around, but I think that the quality of your average opera singer is better than it was.

Then there is the question of stage production, and here we have to recognise the biggest change which has occurred in my years of opera-going. Directors and designers have taken it upon themselves to "interpret"—some would say "misinterpret"—operas to a degree which was inconceivable in the 1960s. In general I consider that the pluses from this have exceeded the minuses. Not everyone will agree, but that is a matter which I prefer to leave until Chapter Nine.

In any event, operamania is not just about performances. It is also about places, journeys, people, happenings, unexpected as well as expected. It can be frustrating, but also it can be great fun, even funny. If you do not believe me, read on.

CHAPTER TWO

OPERA HOUSES AND OTHER VENUES

In April 2005, my wife Helen and I were spending a long weekend in Venice, and on our agenda was a performance of a rare Donizetti opera, *Pia de' Tolomei,* at the famous Teatro La Fenice. Naturally, we were excited, this being our first visit to one of the world's most famous opera houses. One preliminary question was how we should get there from our hotel, because, to say the least, the transport options in Venice are not that conventional. We were smartly dressed—I was wearing my black tie suit—and, at first, it seemed appropriate to arrive in style with a gondola, but I confess that I jibbed at the price that I would have to pay. So it was the *vaporetto*, and a ten-minute walk.

We marvelled at the building: the marble foyer, the beautiful wooden flooring, the elegant staircases, and the red-and-gold auditorium. Regarded as one of the most beautiful theatres in the world, La Fenice had been completely destroyed by a disastrous fire in 1996. It later transpired that two electricians had been threatened with penalty payments for being late with their work on some fittings, and they had spread petrol around the building and set fire to it. They were sentenced to six and seven years' imprisonment, respectively.

Our performance was during the first season of opera since reconstruction. *Fenice* means *phoenix* and this seemed so apt given the horrendous problems of rebuilding a large old theatre in the middle of

Venice. To hold the crane necessary for the work, a special support, with pillars and reinforced concrete, had to be embedded in the bottom of a canal. There was not enough space on the site to produce the cement and this had to be transported through pipes from a pontoon located in the Grand Canal. The work is estimated to have cost some £60 million, but with a treasure like La Fenice, what alternative was there?

Before the performance we enjoyed a *prosecco* in the bar and that allowed us an opportunity to view how members of the audience were dressed. We were in the minority in having formal attire, but nevertheless we marvelled at some stunning female gowns of the kind one might only see in Italy or France. Although there were some foreign tourists like ourselves, most of the audience appeared to be local and were clearly treating the outing as a social, as well as a cultural, event.

Then we went to find our seats. I had secured two tickets at sixty euros each, through an agency because it had been difficult to obtain them directly from the theatre. At that price—remember it was 2005—I thought that they must be reasonably good; but *orrore!* they were in fact the worst seats I have ever had for a theatrical performance anywhere. We had two rear chairs in a box at the very side of the auditorium. From that position, I could not see anything of the stage at all, since I was facing the audience; if I stood, I could see about one-fifth of the performing area. The two people occupying the front seats, foreigners like ourselves, sympathised with our plight, but did little to enable us to have a better view. In desperation, I searched for an usherette on whom I vented my anger. She was embarrassed and said that she would try to find better seats for us after the First Act. She did, and for Acts Two and Three we had front seats in a box facing the stage. So, in the end, we were lucky; pity that, after all this hassle, the performance of the Donizetti was not extraordinary.

Over the years, I have seen opera in a variety of venues, from the glamour of La Fenice at one extreme to open-air arenas and factories at the other. Of course, many of the performances have been in "opera houses", theatres specifically designed for opera with, notably, an orchestra pit. There are very few in this country, the Royal Opera House Covent Garden being the most prominent example; but they are frequently encountered in continental Europe and the explanation is clear. Historically, opera has played a more central role in the culture of Italy, Germany and Central Europe than in our own. In the nineteenth century, each principality, which geographically might be quite small, would have its own court opera and in modern times the tradition has been perpetuated by municipalities.

When we think of opera houses, certain images of a glitzy building like that of La Fenice come to mind: a horseshoe-shaped auditorium with chandeliers, crimson upholstery, and rows of private boxes; and, surrounding it, spacious foyers, elegant staircases and sophisticated (and expensive) bars. The most famous European opera houses, such as La Scala Milan, the Liceu Barcelona, and the Vienna Staatsoper, conform to this pattern.

The design of these grand opera houses may be said to reflect their social function as much as the promotion and appreciation of musical theatre. Take the boxes which are the predominant form of seating outside the stalls and the uppermost galleries. The reasons for their dominance are clear. The moveable chairs within a box enable even the most heavily gowned females to sit and stand with ease. The independent space allows for the entertainment of visitors during the intervals and maybe even during the performance; and the relative privacy might, when the lights are down, facilitate activities which are not entirely related to spectating. When the lights are up, the occupants of boxes are visible to much of the rest of the audience, so that who is accompanying whom can be easily observed and commented on. Perhaps, then, it is not surprising that my seat in La Fenice faced the auditorium rather than the stage, because, at least in past ages, its occupants might have been more interested in observing who was in the theatre, with whom, and what they were wearing.

Social interaction in the auditorium may be less common in modern times, but the spaces outside it—the foyers, wide corridors, bars and refreshment halls—are clearly still important in some opera houses for showing off dresses, meeting friends and colleagues, attending receptions for corporate sponsors, or simply revealing one's presence. During the intervals at some German opera houses, in the 1960s and 1970s, I remember that well-dressed couples would, once they had consumed their *sekt* (sparkling wine), parade arm in arm, nodding to their acquaintances as though in some military ceremony.

In the summer of 2010 I was in Altenburg, a small town in Thuringia and best known for the fact that it was there that skat, a popular card game in Germany and a favourite pastime of Richard Strauss—it features in his "domestic" opera *Intermezzo*—was invented; playing cards are also manufactured there. Much of the town is in a state of decay, the result of continuing neglect during the German Democratic Republic era. But, right in the centre, is a little gem, an opera house, dating from 1870 and now beautifully restored. I saw there a traditional but enjoyable production of Lortzing's comic opera *Zar und Zimmermann*. The square in which the theatre stands has undergone several changes of names in the last century, an indicator of the political upheavals which it has witnessed. In 1920 it was *Theaterplatz*, but in 1933 became *Adolf-Hitler-Platz*, then in 1947 *Rosa-Luxemburg-Platz*, before in 1990 it was allowed to return to its original name.

Throughout its history, this opera house must have been a symbol not only of the German obsession with culture, but also of political power and privilege. Its very existence and prominence are explained by the fact that it stands at the foot of the castle in which resided the Duke of Saxe-Altenburg. It was, therefore, connected to the court, serving principally the interests and tastes of the local aristocracy, and of course that is reflected in the structure of its interior with its royal box, and the attendant luxury of its fittings. When, however, in central and eastern Europe, the ruling nobility responsible for these beautiful theatres were overthrown by revolutionary forces, what would happen to the symbols of the *ancien regime*? Mostly, they were, to a greater or lesser extent, preserved. But the more interesting question is how the luxurious fittings and arrangements, designed to reinforce social elitism, could be reconciled with the new political doctrine.

Although that would not seem to be a problem for fascist regimes, what about socialist regimes which espoused egalitarianism? No doubt the political masters were able to convince themselves that pre-revolutionary art forms, including opera, could be seen as part of an evolutionary path towards the ideal socialist future, but that could not easily be applied to the buildings designed to enhance class differences. Because of such anachronisms, opera-going behind the old Iron Curtain was a fascinating experience.

I made my first visit to East Berlin in 1975. At that time, the lovely little Komische Oper, tucked away in Behrenstrasse, just off the Unter den Linden boulevard, was a "must" for opera enthusiasts. This was because its Artistic Director Walter Felsenstein (he died later the same year) and his disciples, including Joachim Herz, were responsible for some of the most imaginative and exciting music theatre productions of the period. But East Berlin was a grim place. Getting there was itself an unpleasant experience with long waits at the Friedrichstrasse station crossing point where I had to undergo undignified body searches. When at last I emerged into the street, the city was deserted; I felt almost alone in the elegant Unter den Linden, an extraordinary contrast to the crowded thoroughfare one finds today.

I walked then to the Komische Oper to seek a ticket for a performance of Felsenstein's famous production of Britten's *Midsummer Night's Dream* which was to be given that evening. Standing next to the box office window was a burly individual—presumably a party official—instructing the woman responsible for selling the tickets as to what seats she should select for whom. And when it was my turn, I was placed on the very edge of the auditorium, heedless of my request for something more central (*"im Zentrum, bitte"*).

Notwithstanding my disappointing vantage point, I enjoyed the excellent performance. Although Britten's musical depiction of the fairy world was made unattractively heavy by a baritone Oberon (counter-tenors had not, apparently, reached East Germany at that time), the production was light and brilliantly inventive, a feature which I sensed was insufficiently appreciated by a rather staid audience. Applause was polite, rather than enthusiastic. Perhaps the spectators who presence had been approved by the burly party official were not necessarily those most responsive to twentieth-century opera, even though they certainly enjoyed the experience of being in this pretty little theatre.

A year later, in 1976, I was in Bratislava with a female companion, Catherine. In truth our visit to that city had been very stressful. The clampdown on freedom by the Soviet-installed regime, following the 1968 events in Czechoslovakia and the Russian invasion, was still very tight. We had planned to stay with the parents of a Slovak friend then studying in Oxford. We were warmly received by the couple, but immediately told that it was not a good idea to speak in the apartment as there were certainly microphones in the walls (both of them had been active in the "Prague Spring"). Furthermore, we should not stay with them, as suspicions were aroused by Western visitors. So we were taken to a hotel. On the way there we passed the house in which Alexander Dubček, the famous leader who had attempted to liberalise the regime, was allowed, under supervision, to live. We saw also the police cars which were constantly parked outside. When we arrived at the hotel, we found it to be old fashioned and spacious, but in poor condition—there were no plugs in the bathroom and we could have hot water only at certain hours in the day.

Of course we wanted to visit the Opera, and we discovered that *Fidelio* was being given that evening, although in a "closed" performance which could be attended only by local schoolteachers. Fortunately, one of our hosts, who had been a journalist before she was dismissed for her anti-socialist activities, knew everybody who was anybody in Bratislava and prided herself on her ability to "beat the system". So, after she had had a quick chat with the box office manager and an usherette, we were inside and found empty seats at the back of the stalls; this was not difficult because the theatre was only one third full.

The Slovak National Theatre responsible for the performance is now housed in a remarkable new building opened in 2007, but in 1976 we were at the "old" theatre, a traditional opera house. This was built in 1885 by Helmer and Fellner, famous Viennese architects who had designed a number of opera houses in central Europe, including the Vienna Staatsoper, the Berlin Komische Oper, described above, as well as those in Budapest, Prague and Odessa.

Clearly the Bratislava theatre had seen better days. The curtain was almost threadbare and the upholstery of the seats was much in need of renewal. Throughout the building there was an atmosphere of drabness and gloom reflecting conditions in Czechoslovakia generally at the time. And yet, the performance of Beethoven's opera was an electrifying one which seemed to shake the theatre as much as it shook us.

This was not because the singers were particularly good—they were in fact too old for their roles and their voices were strained. The chorus were no younger and lacked power and precision. Certainly the quality of the staging helped: it was imaginative in its movement and had strikingly large and oppressive sets. But it was above all the intensity of the musical interpretation which communicated itself to us. The conductor Zdeněk Košler, the soloists and chorus, whatever their limitations, all obviously felt, and wanted to express for themselves, Beethoven's cry for freedom in a way which in other contexts was not possible. Afterwards Catherine and I walked through the empty streets of Bratislava too moved to speak. In some way that performance of *Fidelio* in the drab old opera house cemented our relationship, for we were soon to agree to live together and subsequently to marry.

It has to be said that, for genuine music lovers, the traditional nineteenth-century opera house has definite disadvantages. If you cannot afford a seat in the stalls or in a box from which one has a decent view of the stage, the likelihood is that you will be in an upper gallery. You may then be obliged to enter the theatre by an entrance separate from that used for the lower parts of the house, no doubt because it was not deemed appropriate for the poorer classes to mix with those who could afford the more expensive seats. There is a long climb up a stairway bare of carpets and ornamentation. Once you get to your seats, you will probably find that there are spectators sitting in the front row who have the irritating habit of leaning over the rail, preventing you having a decent view of the stage. If these circumstances occur in Britain, I usually have the courage to tap the offender on the shoulder and ask if they will be kind enough to sit back. But my effort to do likewise in a foreign opera house—was it in Strasbourg or Liège?—was met with a combination of bewilderment and hostility, and I have rarely ventured to repeat the experiment.

From considerations of comfort and visibility, then, it seems natural to bless the design of modern opera houses, where you can see and hear reasonably well from almost any part of the theatre—I will return to them later in this chapter. But is something lost in terms of atmosphere and tradition? I have much nostalgia for my opera-going days at Covent Garden in the 1960s, not the least for the amphitheatre (what would be the upper gallery in most theatres) and which was the only place with seats at prices which I could then afford. When you had survived the long climb up the stairs from the rather austere entrance in Floral Street, there was something reassuringly intimate about the small cloakroom where your coat was hung, the unpretentious bar where you could buy a cup of coffee and a biscuit, and the stall where the friendly lady sold you the inexpensive programme.

Suitably fortified by the coffee, you would enter the auditorium and then brace yourself for the discomfort of sitting on cramped benches, a hardship imposed on impecunious opera enthusiasts before the top rows of the amphitheatre were redesigned in 1964 and conventional seats installed. But the very discomfort created a camaraderie among the bench occupants, many of whom were knowledgeable and easily induced into operatic chats and reminiscences.

The benches in the upper amphitheatre were not the only possibility if your resources were limited. There were also the Upper Slips, in the highest points of the auditorium, both left and right. The tickets for these were even cheaper, but you could not see too much of the stage from up there. The fact that the sound was good encouraged some young people, presumably music students, to sit in front of a little lectern helpfully provided by the management, so that, with the aid of a little light, they could follow the score of the work being performed.

However, a much better option was to purchase a ticket at a very modest price (was it seven shillings?) to stand at the rear of the Stalls Circle. I did this when I first saw Wagner's *Ring* in the Solti–Hotter production of 1965, and although physically it was a bit of an ordeal I felt immensely privileged to have had such a good vantage point for this memorable operatic "first". The problem with the standing system, at that time, was that tickets would only be available a couple of hours before the performance, and then only if all seats in the house had been sold.

When it comes to standing places at opera houses, it has to be admitted that there is no better system than that operating at the Vienna Staatsoper where the *Stehplätze,* as they are known, and their occupants are as much a part of the tradition of the theatre as the promenaders at London's Albert Hall. Most of the *Stehplätze* are located at the back of the stalls and there you can lean on helpfully provided railings, rather like those used at football stadiums in this country when standing was still the norm for spectators.

From the back of the stalls, the sound and view of the stage are both excellent. Moreover, there are no less than 540 *Stehplätze* available (though not all in the stalls) and tickets are sold at a very modest price on the day of the performance, however many seats remain unsold. At my first visit to the Staatsoper in 1976, for a performance of *Les Contes d'Hoffmann* (with a typically Viennese stellar cast) I happily occupied a *Stehplatz*, but when, at the end of the First Act, I spotted an empty seat just in front, I glided into it. I then felt a hand on my shoulder and a not-so-friendly usher barked at me *"nicht gestattet"* (not allowed). You can't have both your Viennese *Küche* and eat it at the Staatsoper.

Beyond the traditional nineteenth-century opera house and its modern, functional equivalent, there are other possible performing venues, some more suitable than others, depending on the piece that is being given and the style adopted for the production. There are still in existence a few theatres built during the eighteenth century and which can be perfect settings for baroque operas. For example, in Munich there is the exquisite Cuvilliés theatre, designed in the rococo style. Mozart's *Idomeneo* was first performed there, and it must surely be ideal for Gluck and even Handel. Unfortunately, the only opera I have ever seen there was *Simplicius Simplicissimus*, a strident anti-militarist and anti-Nazi twentieth-century piece by Karl Amadeus Hartmann; and this was completely at odds with the theatre's architecture, its floral decorations and its carvings.

More satisfying was my visit to the Drottningholm Palace Theatre near Stockholm, and the base for a summer festival each year. Built a decade or so later than the Cuvilliés theatre, it is equally ornate, but smaller and therefore more intimate. The setting for Rossini's comedy *Pietra del Paragone*, which I saw there, is an aristocratic country house, and both the drama and the music accorded perfectly with the surroundings; indeed the theatre became, in a sense, part of the performance.

The prime example of congruity between a theatre and opera performed there must nevertheless be the Festspielhaus at Bayreuth. Over a period of more than forty years, I have been to it for six festivals, comprising sixteen performances (including three complete cycles of the *Ring*). Unquestionably, my first visit in 1967 was the most memorable, no doubt in part because of the novelty of the experience. Arriving in the northern part of the town of Bayreuth, you soon see the famous large, light brown building looming out of the trees at the top of a green hill (the legendary *Grüne Hügel)*. However much you may have read, or heard, about the theatre, it cannot fail to make a big impact when you see it in the flesh for the first time. This is not so much due to the atmosphere created by the multitude of people in formal dress (still worn by most festival-goers) milling about, nor the expectation of the performance to come, fuelled by the brass players emerging onto the balcony fifteen, ten and five minutes before the start, to play leitmotifs from the opera. It is rather when you enter the theatre.

There are no fancy carpets, no gilt staircases, no bars or refreshment rooms. You enter almost immediately into the auditorium and there you get your first surprise, for unlike almost any other nineteenth-century theatre, there are no boxes, or "privileged" seating. Instead, as in a Greek amphitheatre, which was the model for the design, all spectators are treated with equal respect and you can see and hear perfectly even from the cheaper seats, which are admittedly at some distance from the stage.

You now begin to understand the success of Wagner's mission to replace the conventional opera house by one in which the audience is there not to interact socially but rather to engage wholly with the drama and the music. In most nineteenth-century theatres it is easy for the eyes to wander to the boxes at the side of the auditorium, unsurprisingly since many spectators would want to see who was present. At Bayreuth, there are only pillars framing the fan-like seating area and these are so designed that they direct visual attention towards the stage.

The most original, and most satisfying, feature of the Festspielhaus, and that which strikes you immediately the lights are lowered and the orchestra plays the prelude, is the extraordinary acoustic quality of the building, its clarity and resonance. This is due mainly to the absence of materials which, in most theatres, serve to absorb the sound, such as carpets, the upholstery of the seats and the plush surroundings to the boxes. Then when the singing begins, you get another surprise. In most opera houses there is the problem for singers to project their voices above the sounds from the large orchestra required for Wagner's music dramas. At Bayreuth, there is an almost perfect balance between the singers and the orchestra. This is because a wooden shell covers the front of the orchestra pit, and the sound is thus projected not towards the auditorium but backwards towards the stage, where it blends with the singers' voices.

The Festspielhaus was built between 1872 and 1875. The Paris Opéra was completed during the same period, but in terms of architectural style the two buildings could not be more different. The Paris theatre is often referred to as the Palais Garnier, after the architect Charles Garnier who designed it, and indeed it is palatial. Its massive neo-baroque exterior dominates the ninth arrondissement. And when you enter, you are overwhelmed by its opulence: marble friezes, statues, and chandeliers intermingle with staircases, corridors, and alcoves. You have the feeling that you are in some gigantic royal residence or museum. The auditorium is traditional but heavy. You look up and see an enormous chandelier, but beyond it you get the shock of the Chagall ceiling which, with its flying figures and blue, green, red and yellow splashes, is completely at odds with the heavy gilt surrounds to the stage and seating.

In short, the Opéra Garnier is a monument. When I first attended performances there in the mid-1960s, the artistic stagnation of what was offered on the stage seemed to reflect this: ill-prepared revivals of hammy, old-fashioned productions. The appointment of a new artistic director in 1973, Rolf Liebermann, the Swiss composer and administrator of the Hamburg Opera, turned the Paris Opéra into a vibrant cultural institution, with adventurous productions and an interesting repertory. But in subsequent visits, I still felt that there was something anachronistic about the building and what was performed there. One can see how it might have suited old-fashioned French grand opera which has large numbers on the stage and elaborate decor. Indeed, I experienced this opera house at its best when in 1985 I saw an extravagant (in every sense) production of Meyerbeer's rarely-staged heroic opera *Robert le Diable.* For more conventional operatic fare, and particularly for twentieth-century works, it seemed to provide the wrong environment.

When I went to Lyon in 1973 to attend a performance of *Les Trois Souhaits,* a modernist piece with elements of jazz by the Czech composer Martinů, I had the same problem as at the Palais Garnier. The character of the work and the production given of it were out of place in a nineteenth-century opera house, with its heavy exterior and traditional auditorium.

In the 1980s, the decision was made to gut the building, inserting a modern interior but retaining the exterior; although, to enhance the technical facilities, a steel and glass barrel vault was erected above it. Whether this combination of old and new works I cannot tell, since I have not been back to the theatre for a performance. In contrast, the Mitterrand government, under pressure to establish an alternative to the Palais Garnier more in keeping with forward-looking French cultural ideas, found the resources to build a second opera house in Paris.

Opened in 1989, the Opéra Bastille is, indeed, startlingly different from the Palais Garnier. In the first place, it does not have a strong presence in the locality. It is hemmed in at a corner of the Place de la Bastille and its external face makes you feel that it is very much part of an urban landscape, with its white cubes on top of slim pillars, and, in front, a relatively modest flight of steps leading to a simple, but large, marble gateway. Inside the auditorium, the contrast with the traditional opera house is even more pronounced. Instead of luxurious crimson curtains and upholstery, there is clinical white brick combining with orange-brown wood. All the seats, in black velvet, are identical with plenty of leg room and excellent views of the stage.

My first performances there, *The Marriage of Figaro* in December 1990 and Berio's *Un Re in Ascolto* in February 1991 revealed both the strengths and limitations of the building. The Mozart was a revival of a famous production of Giorgio Strehler, mounted in 1973 to inaugurate the Liebermann era at the Palais Garnier. Although the cast included a delectable young Cecilia Bartoli as Cherubino, the staging with its intimate lighting effects and mellow brown and yellow sets and costumes, seemed ill-adapted to the modernity of the Opéra Bastille. In contrast the production of the Berio opera, a piece loosely based on Shakespeare's *The Tempest*, was full of brilliant stagecraft with acrobats, magicians and dancers, and felt so right in this theatre.

The Opéra Bastille, designed by Carlos Ott, was one of a number of high-profile architectural attempts to find new solutions to the performing of opera in the late twentieth century. In some cities, for example, Oslo,

Sydney and Toronto, there had not been a conventional opera house and the aim was partly to establish a new tradition for opera performances. In others, such as Copenhagen and Paris, there was a desire to break away from the image of the traditional opera house as a preserve of the wealthy, often elderly, bourgeoisie, and to attract new and perhaps younger audiences. In either case, there was also a concern to provide better visibility and acoustics, and to enhance the environmental setting for opera-going. Less obviously desirable, but just as common, was the huge cost of the buildings, typically overrunning their budgets by a long way, and giving rise to major political squabbles.

Although not so much noticed outside Germany, the Aalto-Oper in Essen has provided a model of what can be done. Because it is located in the Ruhr basin, and is the home of the Krupp steel industry, Essen has unfairly acquired the reputation of being a rather unattractive place. In fact it is a pleasant city with an excellent art museum and a rich cultural life. Already in 1959 the Finnish architect Alvar Aalto had drawn up plans for a new opera house, but work on it did not begin until 1983, seven years after his death, and five more years passed before the theatre was opened.

The wait was worthwhile. As you approach the building, you are at once aware of irregular shapes and curves rising into the sky, the brilliant whiteness of the stone contrasting with the dark strips of windows, thus giving the impression of an elongated keyboard. The irregularity is maintained in the auditorium, the upper levels of seating projecting at odd angles, their light gold framework nicely complementing the indigo-blue seats. And when you sit down, there is ample room to stretch out your legs, the distance between the rows of seating apparently facilitating the excellent acoustics. Needless to add, you have a good view of the stage from even the cheapest seats. In short, merely being at the Aalto-Oper is an agreeable experience and puts you in a positive frame of mind for appreciating musical theatre; and the environment works for a wide range of opera, since I have seen works as diverse as those by Vivaldi and Wagner successfully performed there.

While little is heard of the Aalto-Oper outside its own country, the opposite is true of the Sydney Opera House. Understandably this project attracted much publicity from the beginning. The winner of the competition, the Danish architect Jørn Ultzon, had gone for a design which was radical at the time. Several technical problems arose during construction and it took seventeen years before the project was finally completed in 1973, with an escalation of the cost to some $120 million, a huge sum for that period. Attempts by the New South Wales Government to reduce some of the expenditure led to the architect's resignation in 1966, and he was to die before the building was opened.

But the most lasting problem arose from a change of plan concerning usage. The term "opera house" is somewhat of a misnomer, because it is in fact an arts complex, containing five performance halls. The largest of these had been intended for opera, but the government decided that, given its capacity, it would better serve as a concert hall. In consequence the stage was concreted over, and the proscenium arch was removed, as was the tower required for theatrical machinery. Opera was banished to a smaller hall, a far from satisfactory solution since a full orchestra, as needed for works by Strauss and Wagner, could not fit into the pit there.

So what were my impressions when in 2001 I visited the venue for a performance by Australian Opera of Puccini's *Trittico*? True, the architecture makes a huge impact as you approach Sydney harbour. The site juts out into the water and the differently-sized concrete shells rise into the sky like the unfurled sails of a ship. Once you have marvelled at this image and walked through the pleasant surrounds of the buildings, you enter the complex. I did not visit the larger auditorium which is, apparently, impressive, but I have to say that the opera theatre was a little disappointing. The auditorium is attractive and comfortable but contains nothing unusual. The acoustics were not great and, whether or not influenced by my knowledge of the history of the place, I could understand the feeling that, in relation to the concert hall, it might indeed be the "poorer cousin".

Poverty was far from my mind when I experienced the new Oslo opera house in 2009. The setting has some similarities with Sydney: it too is built in a harbour and the interaction between its design (by the Norwegian firm Snøhetta) and the water is important, but the exterior of the building presents an image not of ships, but rather of a glacier. The roof is mainly flat, sloping gently upwards, while the pedestrian walkways surrounding it tilt towards the fjord. You enter through a crevice below the roof, and immediately get a sense of height and light from the huge windows. The foyer seems to be all white diagonals, columns, walls and ceiling, and this contrasts most effectively with an internal circular wooden wall framing a corridor around the auditorium. Having admired all of this, and enjoyed an excellent fish meal in the restaurant on the ground floor, I found that what followed was something of an anticlimax. The auditorium was, in contrast to the rest of the project, traditional in shape and design. And the production, which was of Puccini's *Fanciulla del West*, relied on the hackneyed ideas of presenting the piece as a glamorous Hollywood musical western. I suppose that, as with most things, you cannot be perfectly satisfied with everything.

In the warmer climates of continental Europe it is possible, during the summer, to have open-air performances of opera, and there are a number of famous locations where these take place. Of course, appropriate weather cannot be guaranteed and, if it rains, the performance may be cancelled or else transferred to an indoor venue—I have experienced both outcomes.

Bad weather is rarely a problem in Italy in the summer months, and I first went to the Verona Roman arena in 1967. At that time, you did not book a ticket in advance, unless you wanted a "proper seat" in the central section of the arena. You simply turned up on the day and paid one thousand or two thousand lire, depending on where on the stone terraces you wanted to sit. When I returned in 1989 things were very different. By then it had become a major tourist attraction, with groups of visitors arriving from all over Europe, and tickets were not always easy to come by.

I have to confess that I have generally been disappointed by opera *al fresco*. This is partly a question of sound. Although the voices in some arenas, such as Verona, can carry remarkably well, they tend to disappear into the atmosphere, and in many locations amplification is used. But more importantly it is a question of what, for lack of a better term, I can call "theatricality". We all know how a film watched in a darkened cinema has a much greater impact than when seen on the television in the sitting room. Similarly, where a performance is given within an enclosed space, separated from the audience either by structures such as a proscenium arch, or by lighting effects which can accentuate the players and the action, the drama can entirely absorb your attention in a way that is rarely possible out of doors. This is particularly the case if you are continually distracted by people taking flash photos, a problem which, in my experience, has marred many open-air opera performances. While flash photography may in theory be prohibited, in practice there is little that can be done to stop it.

Admittedly, open-air performances tend to have compensating features. In Verona it is impressive when, before the performance starts, the arena is darkened so that the spectators may light the little candles which they have bought for the purpose. Then, at a performance of *Nabucco* on my second visit, the conductor turned round to the audience to lead them in singing the Chorus of the Hebrew Slaves—a big sound with an audience of 15,000.

But the main attraction must be the opera itself. Provided that the work is appropriate for this treatment, the production, particularly in Roman arenas, can aim at the spectacular, with massive sets, a large chorus, and hundreds of extras, including animals. The highlight of *Aida* at the Terme di *Caracalla* at Rome, when I was there in 1964, was the appearance of dozens of horses and chariots for the Triumphal March, of course greeted by huge applause.

Monumental, traditional stagings of this kind do not often add much to the drama. But on occasions the opportunities presented by open-air performances can, with technological aids, be so imaginatively exploited that the effect is stunning. The summer opera festival at Bregenz on Lake Constance provides a good example. In 2009 I saw there an *Aida* which, as mounted by the British artistic team of Graham Vick and Paul Brown, was very different from what I had experienced in Rome.

Across from the wooden terraces holding about 7000 spectators was a floating stage, above which, for this event, were two huge cranes. As part of the production, these carried into the performing space symbols relevant to a drama about war and suppression, including a damaged Statute of Liberty. At another point, a gunboat surged away on the water, carrying Radames and his fellow soldiers to war. The magnificent climax of the evening was a vessel containing the dying lovers hoisted into the night sky, and presumably heaven; not what Verdi prescribed as the ending, but true to the spirit of the work.

In terms of its theatrical impact, *Aida* in Bregenz may have been exceptional for open-air opera—it is rumoured that something like £10 million was spent on the production. But two other festivals I have attended show how it is possible to reach a satisfactory compromise between a conventional theatre and a performance space which is totally open to the elements. Both Aix-en-Provence and Santa Fé in New Mexico are hot in mid-summer, and it is pleasant to be outside in the evening. The Théâtre d'Archevêché in Aix and the Opera House in Santa Fé are in the open air, but there is roofing for the performers and the audience. The result is not only better acoustics, because the roofing shields the sound and sends both voices and orchestra towards the audience; it also frames the dramatic action and thus creates a more contained and intimate environment for the work, so that the concentration of the audience can be secured. This is helped by the fact that the performing space is not large and so these venues have proved to be ideal for smaller scale works, such as those by Mozart and Rossini.

For understandable reasons, there has not been much open-air opera in Britain (the stagings in the Deanery garden at Bampton constitute a courageous exception), but we have our own version of festive opera.

This may perhaps be termed "country house" opera and, of course, has its origin and inspiration in Glyndebourne. Founded in the 1930s by John Christie, a wealthy and eccentric opera enthusiast, it has, without a penny of public subsidy, had a phenomenal success. It is not difficult to understand why. The combination of the setting, the lovely rolling countryside of the South Downs, the attractive house, with its gardens, lawns and walks, the long dinner interval when—weather permitting— you can enjoy a stylish picnic; and the atmosphere created by a well-dressed group of people having a half-day away from urban life with all its preoccupations. There is also the intimacy of the place: I have resisted the temptation to renew my long-neglected prowess on the croquet lawn but, like many others, have regularly visited the Organ Room with its family portraits and other memorabilia.

All of this would be insufficient were the performances not of high quality; and in my experience the artistic standards at Glyndebourne have been, with only very few exceptions, extremely high. This has been a consequence partly of first-rate artistic management, selecting outstanding singers, conductors and directors whose talents are well suited to the works to be performed; and partly of meticulous preparation, facilitated by the team working together over a number of weeks in a pastoral retreat, far from other distractions.

In the days of the old theatre, before it was demolished and replaced by the new building in 1994, the repertory rightly centred on Mozart, early nineteenth-century works and some twentieth-century pieces, such as Debussy's *Pelléas et Mélisande* and Britten's *Albert Herring* which could be appropriately accommodated within the limited space. But Glyndebourne was also pioneering, venturing into the field of early opera at a time when it was by no means popular. Under the tutelage of Raymond Leppard, and with the colourful stagings of Peter Hall, there were some delightful revivals of Monteverdi pieces and the exciting discovery of works by his Venetian contemporary, Francesco Cavalli.

As one grows older, one tends to become increasingly nostalgic for things as they were, rather than for things as they have become; and I have to admit that I miss very much the old Glyndebourne theatre. Its seating capacity was limited and its acoustics were not wonderful, but it had an intimacy, a proximity between audience and performers, that reflected the "family" character of the festival. I do not like the style of the new theatre: for me, its architect Michael Hopkins tried too hard to create a "modern" small version of a traditional opera house.

But with the rebuilding came other, positive changes. The repertory could be extended into larger-scale works, so that even Wagner is now performed there, including, in 2011, the massive *Meistersinger*. The increased size of the auditorium has also meant that tickets are not now so hard to come by; and that in turn has given rise to a less exclusive and more varied audience.

The festival has always attracted visitors, including the guests of corporate sponsors, whom it would be reasonable to assume are not regular opera-goers. In the old days, one could sense in some fellow members of the audience a lack of attentiveness and occasional boredom in, for example, a Mozart/Da Ponte opera, because they could not understand sufficiently well what was being sung. The arrival of surtitles changed that and, as in other opera houses, audiences have become more engaged.

In general, the social and cultural aspects of the festival complement each other very well. I have been to Glyndebourne alone only once and although the performance (Rossini's *Ermione* in an excellent production by Graham Vick) was as good as almost any other I have attended there, the experience was not so enjoyable. Sharing the champagne and picnic with others adds to one's pleasure and does not detract from the satisfaction to be had from high-class artistic endeavours. You treat the occasion as something special, and when you arrive and are charged what seems like an exorbitant sum for the programme and for a cup of tea and a piece of cake, you just shrug your shoulders and murmur "what the hell!".

The Glyndebourne phenomenon has been much imitated. In recent years, the owners of some English country houses have created theatres of sorts in or around their buildings and have established summer opera festivals there, with well-dressed audiences picnicking in a dinner interval and revelling in picturesque surroundings. For some reason, they have proliferated in and around the Cotswolds, with Garsington and Bampton in Oxfordshire, Longborough in Gloucestershire, and Iford near Bath. But there is also Grange Park in Hampshire which, since it is conveniently close to where members of my family live, I have visited three times.

The first two occasions could not have been more contrasting. The first in 2008 was in atrocious weather. Under incessant rain we slithered from the car park to the house, and not even the stoutest umbrella could prevent a damp transfer from auditorium to the (thankfully) covered picnic place. But the performance of Dvorak's *Rusalka* was superb: a picture-book production, capturing both the fantasy and the inner tensions of the work. The following year, the weather was much better but the performance was abysmal. In its British première, Cavalli's *Eliogabalo* was given such a silly, vulgar production that we hardly noticed the music.

In November 2008, I turned up at the Opera House in Duisburg half an hour before a performance of Wagner's *Rheingold* was due to begin. I was dismayed to find that nothing was happening in the theatre and that there were only a few people outside. My first thought was that the performance had been cancelled, but there was no notice pinned to the theatre doors to this effect, as would be normal in such circumstances. So I asked one of the passers-by and was told that the opera was being given not in the theatre but in the *"Kraftzentrale"*, something I could have discovered for myself if I had examined my ticket carefully. Apparently this place was too far away to reach on foot, so I hired a taxi and was taken into the industrial outskirts of the town, there to be dropped outside what appeared to be an industrial museum complex. Indeed, this was the case, and I soon found that the performance was to be given in an abandoned factory.

In the middle of the factory was the orchestra and, on either side, banked seats, occupying, rather strangely, only about one third of the available space. During the performance I discovered why. As the music described the transition from the first scene at the bottom of the Rhine to the mountain tops where Wotan and the other gods lived, as if by magic, our bank of seats slid from one end of the factory where there was a small reservoir of water, to the other filled with large rectangular blocks. But the best moments came when we were moved again for the third scene, where the Nibelungen were busy hammering at the gold to give the dwarf Alberich power over the world. What better symbol of capitalism than the noise of the hammer blows resounding around the factory?

The choice of a factory to present *Das Rheingold* was clearly motivated by a desire to link the work, or its interpretation, to a specific location for which it had associations. Interaction with the industrial setting added to the resonance of the drama. A similar effect can be experienced at the Savonlinna Festival in Finland where opera is performed in the courtyard of a 500-year-old castle. This may give a level of realism to pieces about feudal rivalries set in the middle ages, but was not obviously appropriate for Wagner's *Flying Dutchman* which I saw there and which is set in and around a Norwegian fishing village. However, the backdrop of the grim castle walls worked in a different way. With the ships' rigging and red sails hauled across them, they created an otherworldly atmosphere which suited Wagner's tale of a mysterious traveller.

Then, in the west of London every summer, opera is performed in a tent set against the ruins of Holland House, a seventeenth-century mansion. The festival has developed a reputation for mounting revivals of seldom performed *verismo* operas. In 2007 I saw a particularly effective production of *L'Amore dei Tre Re* by Montemezzi, a melodramatic piece about the love affair of an unhappily married princess. Not the least reason for its success was the visual impact made by her lonely appearance on a grey tower constructed into the ruins of the old house.

Another reason for unusual performance venues is a desire to sever connections with traditional theatres, thereby "freshening" the communication of music and drama and perhaps attracting audiences who might be unwilling to enter opera houses. And the informality of the location can encourage an innovative approach to productions and performance styles, which can be imaginative and exciting. The City of Birmingham Touring Opera, under Graham Vick's direction, has for several years adopted such an approach, performing principally in community centres in the West Midlands. I remember a particularly brilliant presentation of *Zaide*, an unfinished and rarely performed comedy by Mozart, which the Birmingham company brought to Bradford in 1992. With an adaptation of the text by Italo Calvino, Vick turned this otherwise shallow piece into a detective thriller and, with much energetic action on the small playing arena, the results were highly successful.

The financial problems of mounting full-scale productions have led some organisations to create opera studio theatres, containing no more than a hundred or so seats, sometimes surrounding the playing area. Typically there is room, and money, only for a dozen or so orchestral players. There are a number of chamber operas specifically written for forces such as these, but for other, more conventional works, there has usually to be some scaling down of the orchestral parts. The thinner sound tends to spoil the impact of nineteenth-century romantic operas, but for baroque and some modern pieces the loss does not appear to be significant. Cost and the physical capacity of the venue also mean that sets may be rudimentary and costumes limited to simple black attire; but these features can add to, rather than diminish, the immediacy of the experience for audiences.

For an example, take the Royal Northern College of Music at Manchester, which has a deserved reputation for producing outstanding opera singers and whose student performances have sometimes been staggeringly good. In 2001 the College had built a studio theatre and chose to inaugurate the venue with Handel's *Tamerlano*. This was undoubtedly a risky venture. Handel's operas, which are almost entirely composed of recitative and solo arias, can be static affairs and dramatic veracity has to overcome the problem that not a few of the male parts, both heroes and villains, are sung by women. Such features create challenges for performers and audiences in conventional theatres, let alone small intimate performing spaces. But Jennifer Hamilton's production, conceived as a power struggle in some East European country, between characters wearing trench coats and military uniforms, was a riveting affair; and the proximity of performers to the audience generated an intensity which fully matched the music.

Tamerlano is not be confused with *Tolomeo*, another Handel opera which I saw in a studio theatre in Germany a few years later. In Hamburg's Opernloft the small stage is in a café and you sit at tables and can enjoy a beer while watching the performance. Like Vick's Birmingham venture, the aim is to draw a new audience to opera by rendering the occasion more relaxed and the dramatic experience more immediate.

It worked very well when I saw there a one-woman show which was an operatic adaptation of the *Diary of Anne Frank* by the Russian composer Grigori Frid. But my second visit, to see *Tolomeo,* was a complete disaster. No doubt fearing that the audience would be too easily bored by Handelian *opera seria*, the director got his performers to charge around the stage shouting at each other, then stripping off and rolling around in paint. I left during the interval and have since been wondering whether the performance was really as bad as I thought at the time. To my surprise, I have recently found videoed extracts of the production on You Tube and, yes, these confirm that it was that bad. Those responsible for posting the video on the website presumably thought otherwise. Maybe the audiences who go to opera cafés and the like have tastes different from those who frequent opera houses, but I doubt it.

CHAPTER THREE

OPERATIC EXCURSIONS

In November 2005 I received an email from a French colleague, inviting me to give a talk at his research institute in Nancy, and allowing me to choose any Thursday in May or June the following year. The invitation was very welcome. Nancy is an attractive town which I had visited a few times, but I had never been to the Opéra National de Lorraine which is based there and which has a good reputation. I replied, saying that I would be delighted to accept, but that I would need a day or two to check what was compatible with my existing commitments. I then consulted the website of the Nancy Opera and was delighted to find that performances of Berg's *Wozzeck* were being given in June, including one on Thursday the 22nd. So I emailed saying that I could manage to come to Nancy on that day, but that other Thursdays in May or June might be difficult for me.

This arrangement proved to be acceptable to the research institute and I am happy to report that my talk was well received there. More importantly, the performance of *Wozzeck* was excellent: the production by a French team brought out the expressionism in the piece very well; and the cast, mainly German and American singers, were uniformly good. My only problem was a feeling of guilt in having to decline the invitation to join my host and his fellow researchers for dinner after my talk. However, my experience in situations like this has been that foreign colleagues tend to be quite tolerant. Perhaps it is because they are pleased that a visitor takes such an interest in the local cultural scene; or perhaps they find my preferences refreshingly eccentric.

I have been fortunate that my professional life has given me many opportunities to spend time abroad, thereby providing plenty of opera-going possibilities. Sometimes, as in the case of Nancy, the visit is a very short one, enabling me to attend perhaps only a single performance. But often it seems that invitations are for the beginning or end of a week, and then without too much difficulty it is feasible to add a weekend to the trip. Depending on the country in question, that can mean two or even three performances. From this perspective, a weekend which I remember with particular pleasure was in November 2007 in Hessen in Germany.

I had been in Trier, in the Rhine Palatinate, for a meeting that finished at lunchtime on Saturday. I was then able to travel by train to Darmstadt that afternoon for the European première of *Ainadamar*, an opera by the Argentinean-Israeli composer Osvaldo Golijov. Darmstadt, although badly damaged during the Second World War, is an interesting town with some prominent examples of Jugendstil architecture. It also hosts a biennial Festival of New Music (which I visited way back in 1964) and the small opera company based in the city often strays from the mainstream in its choice of works to perform—hence the Golijov work. This was a commentary on the life of the Spanish poet Federico Garcia Lorca. The music, which was contemporary but had a Spanish-Latin American flavour, was attractive, but the production was muddled, largely because the resident choreographer, Mei Hon Lin, had been chosen to direct the piece, and the emphasis on dance was too much of a distraction from the drama.

I stayed overnight in Darmstadt, then took a train for the short journey to the Rhineland city of Mainz. There, on Sunday afternoon at 14.30, I was to attend a matinee of *Lucia di Lammermoor*. Now, it so happened that at 19.30, on the same day, a gala performance of *Rigoletto* was being given at Mannheim, further up the Rhine. I had never seen two full-scale operatic performances in one day, let alone in different towns, and this was a challenge that I felt I could not resist. From the timetable of the Deutsche Bahn, I learned that if I could get from the theatre to Mainz station to catch a train at 17.10, I could reach Mannheim forty minutes later. This would give me time to find a hotel, grab something to eat and get to the theatre before the performance was to begin.

The Mainz station was fifteen minutes walk from the opera house. Recordings of *Lucia* last about one and three-quarter hours; so I calculated that, with an interval of about twenty minutes, I should make the train. The modern-dress production, by Tatjana Gürbaca, was very good, Lucia becoming a victim of a male-dominated society. Seen first as an innocent teenager, riding a wooden hobby-horse, she was then turned into a sex object in a strange world which she could not understand—an excellent performance, incidentally, by the Macedonian soprano, Ana Durlovsky. So I was pleased that I was not obliged to leave before the end, although I did slip out when the singers appeared for their first curtain call.

I was at Mainz station on time, but—oh dear!—the 17.10 train had been cancelled. Catching the next possible connection to Mannheim I arrived there at 18.50. I entered the first hotel that I could find, reserved a room for the night and then rushed off to the theatre. There was only time for a coffee and a *Brötchen*, but somewhat breathless I was in my seat before the lights were lowered.

The hassle proved to be very worthwhile. The Mannheim Opera is, in my experience, rather like Stoke City or Wigan Athletic in the Premier League: it has a higher level of achievement than you would expect, given its resources. Well supported by local audiences, it maintains a first-rate standard of musical and dramatic performance, while avoiding the German fashion for perverse productions (about which more in a later chapter). It relies mainly on its own solid company of singers. For this *Rigoletto*, however, some international stars—Juan Pons (Rigoletto), Andrea Rost (Gilda) and Piotr Beczala (the Duke)—had been engaged. To their credit, they did not coast along, as so often occurs in gala performances, but were fully integrated into the local production, which itself was most impressive—the predominantly white decor designed by Sandra Meurer being particularly striking. In short, an operatic weekend very well spent.

Those keen to see several opera performances within a relatively short period of time will normally satisfy their thirst in big cities like London and New York, which have two companies, Berlin and Vienna which have three or, perhaps best of all from this perspective, Paris which has, in addition to the Opéra Garnier, the Opéra Bastille and the Opéra Comique, often performances at the Théâtre du Châtelet and the Théâtre des Champs-Élysées.

As regards countries where opera excursionists may indulge themselves, Germany offers the widest range of possibilities. The Operabase website reveals that something like one third of all the opera performances in the world take place there. Nevertheless Austria comes top when the measure is performances per head of population (162.9 per million citizens). Britain is in the lowly twentieth position on this scale with only 17.3 performances per million. Italy does not score much better (17th with 19.6) and many will be surprised that the country which is generally regarded as the home of opera should not have more available.

One reason for this is that Italian theatres adopt the *stagione* system, whereby a single work is given a number of performances during a relatively short period, generally three to six weeks. So even in large cities, such as Milan and Rome, you may be there for over a month and still have the opportunity to see only one opera. Under such a system the singers are normally engaged solely for that production and there is no permanent company.

At the other extreme is the repertory system that operates, or used to operate, in most German, Central and Eastern European opera houses. Here a number of productions are accumulated by opera companies and are revived from time to time for perhaps only a few performances. Each year perhaps four or five new productions are added, with an equivalent number being discarded. For visitors, the major advantage of this system is that you can often see a different work each evening of a short stay in the city. And if you are there for longer periods, the tally can be quite impressive. I spent a month at a research institute in Munich in 1977 and saw eight different productions at the Bavarian State Opera, as well as three at the smaller neighbouring Theater am Gärtnerplatz.

The repertory system can only operate effectively if the company has a permanent team of singers and conductors, some of whom are familiar with the production and can give a few performances of it again without too much rehearsal. But that also, of course, constitutes a problem. Productions of some operas, particularly the more popular ones, can remain unchanged in the repertory for many years, the management assuming that there will be a sufficient demand for seats for each revival. The results can be awful. In October 2000 I went to Düsseldorf to see *Zar und Zimmermann* by Lortzing, primarily because it was a famous opera which I had never seen. The audience seemed to be made up mainly of white-haired old ladies who clapped enthusiastically after the well-known clog dance. But really there was very little worth applauding that evening. The production was old-fashioned, corny and stale, and the singers, some of them far too old for the parts they played, were clearly under-rehearsed (a sign of this is when they have to keep their eyes on the conductor or need regularly to be prompted by the *souffleur*).

The production of *Zar und Zimmermann* had been in the repertory of the Deutsche Oper am Rhein for sixteen years when I saw it. But for German companies which operate the repertory system this is by no means an extreme example of longevity. I remember well my first visit to Hamburg in 1970. I was on the way back from a holiday in Scandinavia. I was running out of cash and had to choose between staying the night in a hotel or going to the opera. Of course, I opted for the latter, which meant sleeping in the car. The sacrifice would have been worthwhile if the performance had been good. Unfortunately, it was a rather mediocre *Madam Butterfly* in a production which dated from 1966. At the time of writing this, in October 2010, I am in Hamburg for a period of six weeks and am astonished to find that in November the same production is being revived, nearly forty-five years after its first performance.

Very few theatres still operate a strict version of the repertory system whereby a production may be revived for a few performances spread over a season, and enabling a visitor to see four or more different operas in a week. In the countries where that system was previously favoured, as indeed in Britain at the London houses and the regional companies, you now mostly find a compromise between the repertory and *stagione* systems. During a period of, say, six weeks, three or four operas may be performed, one of which might be a new production and others revivals of old productions.

The compromise works well where you get some choice of what you see and where, as in London and Vienna, care is taken that revivals of old productions are properly prepared. But that is not always the case. In some theatres, as we have seen, productions of popular operas can remain in the repertory for a very long time and they can then serve as vehicles for jet-setting star singers who fly in for only a few performances. Those singers will not want an onerous rehearsal schedule, and therefore will be more comfortable with a traditional production style since then their Hamburg Tosca will be much the same as what they have done on the stage in, say, New York or Buenos Aires.

Ironically, new productions in Hamburg are often radical and controversial re-interpretations of familiar works. So, in my many visits to the opera house there—a consequence of having work engagements in the city—my experiences have generally fallen into one of two opposing categories. Either I have had an exciting, if also challenging, evening of a new production (for example, Peter Konwitschny's 2004 staging of Schoenberg's *Moses and Aaron* which was set in a village hall rather than in the Sinai desert), with singers freshly prepared by conductor and stage director, fully engaged and working very hard. Or I have had to sit through an old and rather boring production of a work like the *Barber of Seville*, with the performers cruising through something they know musically very well; and the house assistant director, responsible for reviving the production, unable to recreate any dramatic insights which the original might have generated. The contrast between these two categories is simply too great and does not make for the balanced repertory to which a company like this should aspire. So, for me, the Hamburg Opera has been, like Liverpool in the Premier League, an underperforming organisation whose achievements do not match the level of its resources and local support.

Those visiting continental European opera houses from Britain may well be on a holiday abroad, or perhaps have booked, through one of the specialist agencies, a travel, hotel and opera package. Particularly in the summer, the performances may be part of a festival, designed to attract visitors from afar. I have myself often made such trips, though have avoided booking through agencies and packages. This is partly because the packages tend to include tourist attractions which I do not want, and partly because (perhaps wrongly) I have always assumed that it is cheaper, and more fun, to make the arrangements myself. I have also been happy to attend performances in an opera house's regular season, rather than those taking place under festival conditions, because I have not been convinced that the quality of festival performances always justifies the very high prices which are often charged.

My first experience of a European excursion taking in regular performances was in 1971. I was having an Easter break abroad, driving first to Italy, meeting a friend in Milan, and then travelling back through the Alps to stay with another friend in Göttingen, in the heart of Germany. In Milan, we were fortunate to get tickets at La Scala for the first night of a production of Donizetti's *Maria Stuarda,* then a relative rarity. This was my first visit to perhaps the most famous opera house in the world and, in truth, the old-fashioned production by Margherita Wallmannn was disappointingly conventional. But there were dazzling vocal and dramatic performances by Montserrat Caballé in the title role and Shirley Verrett as Queen Elizabeth.

The parents of my Göttingen friend lived in Hanover and she wanted to show me that town. The fact that Wagner's *Das Rheingold* was being performed there on Friday, the day after my arrival in Göttingen, suggested to me that her proposal—some 120 miles for the return trip—was a good one. Göttingen has no opera company (though it has an annual Handel festival in the summer), but it is close to Kassel which, then and now, has a reputation for interesting and good quality musical theatre. So the following day, Saturday, I suggested that we go to the opera there even though what was being performed, *Das Popgeheuer*, was not known to me. In fact, it was a new piece by a contemporary British composer, Anthony Gilbert, using a combination of pop, classical and electronic music for a modernised version of the Faust legend. When later the work was given at Sadlers Wells, as *The Scene Machine*, it was not well received, but I much enjoyed the Kassel performance which was mounted in an extravagant and somewhat outrageous production.

On Sunday morning, I left my friend (who by then had, I think, exhausted her appetite for opera), and had to decide what I should do in the two days left before getting to the ferry on Tuesday afternoon in Ostend. To my delight, I discovered that *Tristan und Isolde* was being given in Mainz. True, that meant driving some distance (130 miles) south-west, not exactly in the direction of Ostend, but *Tristan* was the only mature opera by Wagner that at the time I had never seen; and the opportunity was unmissable.

Sadly, it turned out to be a huge disappointment. The two principal singers were veterans, physically ample, and well past their best. The music by itself was insufficient to stir my passion, particularly as the local orchestra seemed to be over-extended by the demands of the work. It was a lesson for me: Wagner performances have to be chosen with care and those at smaller theatres are best avoided. Fortunately I was to experience *Tristan* again, only a couple of months later, conducted by Georg Solti at Covent Garden in Peter Hall's superb production.

It was now Monday, and you might have thought that my operatic expedition had come to an end, because that day is not the best for cultural activities. But, lo and behold, I was able, on the way back north, to call in at Düsseldorf, and there to see *The Rise and Fall of the City of Mahagonny* by Bertolt Brecht and Kurt Weill. The company known as the Deutsche Oper am Rhein had a good reputation in the 1970s particularly for performances of twentieth-century works. This production of *Mahagonny* was directed by Bohumil Herlischka, a Czech emigrant, who did much to foster an interest in the works of Janáček in Germany in the post-war period. His staging was a trifle vulgar for my taste—I had vivid memories of Michael Geliot's production at Sadlers Wells, when the work was given its British première in 1963, and this had been truer to the spirit of Brecht. Nevertheless, the appearance of the great Wagnerian Swedish-American singer, Astrid Varnay, in the role of the Mrs Begbick, the dominant female capitalist, was a major compensation and brought my enjoyable trip to a fitting climax.

If you are abroad for some time, you can explore the operatic possibilities at a more leisurely pace. In 1973 I spent a couple of months at the Council of Europe in Strasbourg. Now the Opéra du Rhin at Strasbourg, like other French companies, adopts the *stagione* system, so I could see only two performances there. But Strasbourg is very close to Germany, and some calculations from the road map suggested that, given the speed of travel which I could sustain in my Mini on the splendid *Autobahnen,* I could, in an evening, drive to and from a number of operatic venues.

My favourite was Stuttgart (sixty-eight miles away), because the quality of performances there was very high, particularly of Wagner for whose work I had a huge admiration at the time. Closest were Karlsruhe, Freiburg and Saarbrücken. Up the Rhine was Basle (in Switzerland). Down the Rhine were Mannheim, Darmstadt, Mainz and Wiesbaden; and I could just about make Frankfurt (107 miles) and back. I found my way to all of these opera houses during my two months' stay. Also in reach, though I did not go to them because there was nothing on the programme to interest me at the time, were Pforzheim, Kaiserslautern, Heidelberg, and Zürich.

The planning of operatic excursions has been revolutionised in the last two decades by the arrival of the Internet and electronic communications. Before these developments took place, it was far from easy to find out what was being performed where, and how tickets could be obtained.

Of course there were, and still are, opera magazines which, apart from news and reviews, contain a calendar of events at different locations both at home and abroad. But this is often based on information provided by opera companies at the beginning of the season and cannot always be relied on for accuracy. If you know where to look, newspapers are often a better source of information. In 1973 I used most frequently the German weekly *Die Zeit* which appeared every Thursday and had, in its culture section (*Feuilleton*), a fairly complete list of all performances in German-speaking theatres.

In the days of the Iron Curtain, the listings in *Die Zeit* did not include theatres in East Germany. As I explained in Chapter Two, there were excellent reasons for crossing the border from West Berlin into East Berlin to see opera there, but the lack of information about what was being performed at the Komische Oper and the Staatsoper Unter den Linden was a real problem. I nevertheless discovered a good solution. Before the wall came down, the S-Bahn suburban railway service was run throughout Berlin, East and West, by the East German authorities. I got the impression that, for this reason, no self-respecting West Berliner would use the service, preferring the U-Bahn underground run by the West Berlin government. But in the derelict S-Bahn stations the East Germans would post notices, printed in old-fashioned lettering, giving the programme of theatre performances in East Berlin for the next two weeks. So when I was in West Berlin in 1975 and 1981 I became a regular traveller on the S-Bahn, if only to keep myself informed about operatic possibilities.

This is not to say that the absence of information is in all respects a bad thing. There is, perhaps, some pleasure to be had when you are on your travels and you do not know what operatic performances you will come across—the element of surprise can be fun. For example, during an Italian holiday in August 1997, which had included a couple of performances at the Rossini festival in Pesaro, I stayed overnight in Orvieto, in the heart of Umbria, and chanced upon a small-scale production of *Zanetto*, a one-act opera by Mascagni. The singers were young and unknown to me, but enthusiastically gave of their best—and, like a bird lover "twitching" over a rare sighting, I could go home happy that I had an addition to my list of works seen.

Ten years earlier, I had been invited to a conference in Wroclaw. My wife Catherine and I decided to combine the journey to and from that city with a car tour of some other places in Poland, as well as parts of East Germany which were then unknown to me. On the drive out, I knew that we would have the opportunity to stop at Hanover for *The Fiery Angel*, an exciting modernist work by Prokofiev; and, indeed, it was a brilliant performance both dramatically and musically. But once we were the other side of the Iron Curtain, it would be a matter of luck as to what we would encounter there.

The Polish leg included Krakow, a beautiful city relatively free from World War Two damage, and we there stumbled upon a performance of *My Fair Lady*, given by the local opera company. Admittedly, this cannot be regarded as the most appropriate choice for one's first experience of opera in Poland. Perhaps we should have seen a work by Moniuszko—in fact by a couple of days we missed a performance of *The Haunted Manor* by this composer when we stayed a night in Poznan. But it was interesting to see how an Eastern European would present something as essentially British as *My Fair Lady* and it was charming, if also anachronistic, to hear a Polish rendering of "Why Can't The English Teach Their Children How to Speak?"

I will not dwell on the fact that we made a detour to see Auschwitz to which Catherine's father had been deported but from which he had survived—the impact of this visit was predictably shattering. Less traumatic, but at the time a little frightening, was being stopped by the police for speeding just a few miles short of the border with East Germany. The officer wanted to impose an on-the-spot fine, but by then I had got rid of all of my zlotys. I was told that we had to go back to the nearest town to change some money. This was an unattractive prospect, not the least because I had to reach Dresden the other side of the border within a few hours in order to fulfil the terms of my hotel reservation. As a westerner, I could not hope for much flexibility from my GDR hosts.

Happily Catherine was able to exert her Gallic charm and the policeman let us proceed, to our enormous relief.

Arriving in Dresden, then a pale reflection of the beautiful centre for Saxon art and culture which once existed, the first preoccupation, once we had overcome the bureaucratic obstacle of hotel registration, was to find out what was on offer at the Semper Oper, even then one of the most beautiful opera houses in Europe. *Ariadne auf Naxos* by Strauss and Shostakovich's comic piece, *The Nose*, would provide an unhackneyed and attractive fare for our two evenings in the city, particularly as they were both directed by Joachim Herz, one of the leading figures to have emerged from the East German school of imaginative theatre directors. Although, as I shall relate in another chapter, tickets were difficult to obtain, these were two memorable evenings.

The next stop was Leipzig where we saw a reasonably good *Jenufa*. Performances of this wonderful work by Janáček rarely fail to make an impact, but in truth we were more moved by a visit to the Thomaskirche, where Bach had worked for so many years and for which he had written some of his greatest works. This operatic excursion ended in the attractive city of Weimar, much quieter in 1987 when, unlike today, there were few tourists around. So it was easy to get a room in the Hotel Elephant where Thomas Mann's famous novel on Goethe, *Lotte in Weimar,* was based. The work we caught at the Nationaltheater, where Goethe was once the Director, was not, perhaps, worthy of the literary heritage of the city (Schiller was also a famous resident), being Offenbach's *Orpheus in the Underworld.* This was given in a Germanic but very funny version, and provided a light-hearted ending to a journey which had been both grim and exciting.

IT developments and, in particular, the emergence of the Internet have revolutionised information gathering, and have been a godsend for the opera enthusiast. Now you can get immediate access to the website of each opera house, providing you not only with an up-to-date calendar of performances but also, in most cases, with the facility of purchasing tickets online. There are also general websites covering performances of opera across Europe and beyond. Amongst these, my favourite is Operabase. It provides information about what is being performed by all opera companies, where and when, and, if known, the cast, and artistic team (conductor, director and designer). There is also a link to the website of the company, so that you can confirm that the relevant performance is taking place, as well as obtaining further details. The website has search engines for operas, composers, and individual artists, enabling you to track down where your favourites can be seen.

For committed opera excursionists, Operabase has two other valuable facilities. After the list of dates for performances of a particular opera at a particular theatre, you are given a little calendar tab. Clicking this will give you a list of opera houses within a radius of 125 km and of the works being performed there during the same time period. This is a tremendous aid to planning opera weekends in particular regions. And then, for those who, like me, are keen on seeking out performances of rarely performed works, there is a useful menu of "highlights" for each month, including a list of "rarities", indicating that, for example, in April 2011, you could have seen Stockhausen's *Sonntag aus Licht* in Cologne, Vivaldi's *Farnace* in Paris, Zandonai's *Francesca da Rimini* in Trieste, or Weinberg's *Portrait* in Nancy.

All sources of information are fallible, and cast lists for future performances are notoriously unreliable. If your planned excursion is based on the prospect of seeing a particular singer, you must be aware of the risk that, for some reason or another, the singer will not appear. Of course, this may be for legitimate reasons, such as illness—about which more in another chapter—but some opera companies appear to be relatively relaxed about allowing a singer's name to be given in advance publicity when, presumably, the booking is only provisional, for the name can disappear from subsequent cast lists without any explanation. This is more likely to occur when the opera company in question operates the repertory, rather than the *stagione*, system. Over a season, a role in a given opera may have been allocated to more than one ensemble singer, and changing assignments for particular performances, as the season progresses, enables the company's resources to be used with greater flexibility.

It can happen, then, that the cast which actually gives a performance is very different from that which you might have expected. In December 2003, I was in Leverkusen, an industrial town near Cologne, known more for its football team than for its cultural achievements. I was there to see *Lohengrin* in a visiting performance given by the opera company from Detmold. The programme which I purchased was obviously for all performances by the company of *Lohengrin* that season, and gave double castings for the roles of Lohengrin, Telramund, Ortrud and the Herald. From the list posted at the entrance to the auditorium, I discovered which of the two singers were that evening to perform Lohengrin and Ortrud. But totally new names were given for both Telramund and the Herald, as indeed for two of the Brabant nobles. With all the deletions and additions, the cast list in my programme became almost illegible.

In some special cases, you may have to purchase tickets without any information as to who will sing. This has always been true of the Bayreuth Festival because you enter the ballot for tickets, in the autumn preceding the summer performances, knowing the names only of the conductor, the director and designer responsible for the production. The identity of the singers is generally disclosed in the following spring.

Even this information may be insufficiently precise. When I went to Bayreuth for the first time in 1967, the alternative casting of Ludmila Dvorakova and Birgit Nilsson had been announced for the role of Brünnhilde in the three *Ring* cycles which were being given that year, but without any indication of which of these singers would sing the part in each cycle. The Czech Dvorakova was a fine artist, and had been mightily impressive when she had sung in a performance of *Götterdämmerung* at Covent Garden, which I had attended the previous year. But Birgit Nilsson was, of course, a phenomenon, the leading Wagnerian signer of the post-war period, and although I had seen her *Turandot*, it had been impossible for me to get to her London appearances in Wagner.

I had tickets for the second Bayreuth cycle and was in a state of considerable tension waiting to know who would sing Brünnhilde. Psychologically I have always found it preferable to be pessimistic rather than optimistic, and so I speculated that, as the "junior" of the two singers, Dvorakova would perhaps be allowed the role in the second cycle, sandwiched between Nilsson who would perform the first and third cycles. I seem to recall that the *Besetzungszettel*, the sheet with the cast list to be inserted in the programme, was issued at one o'clock, three hours before the performance of *Die Walküre* was to begin. And I can still relive the thrill of excitement which ran through my body when I discovered the name of Nilsson on that list. The excitement was, incidentally, fully justified. She was amazing, and that was not simply because of the impact made by her powerful voice soaring into the theatre. It was also because of her musical interpretation, her drawing out of nuances from the text, and the conviction of her dramatic portrayal.

I cannot leave the topic of cast lists at the 1967 Bayreuth *Ring* without mentioning the performance of *Götterdämmerung* which I attended. Alongside Nilsson as Brünnhilde, were Wolfgang Windgassen as Siegfried, Josef Greindl as Hagen, and Thomas Stewart as Gunther. Dvorakova had the second soprano role of Gutrune. Martha Mödl, who had sung Brünnhilde at Bayreuth in the 1950s, was a deeply moving Waltraute. And, as a surprise bonus, when it was announced that Anja Silja was ill and would not sing the Second Norn, we learned that her replacement was to be Astrid Varnay, another legendary Bayreuth Brünnhilde. So, on that extraordinary day in August 1967 I heard four Bayreuth Brünnhildes in the same performance. I thus can be forgiven the cliché: you don't get casts like that these days!

My good fortune with the alternative casting in Bayreuth should be contrasted with my experience of *Salome* in Cologne in 2004. I planned to travel from my base in Maastricht (some fifty-five miles away) for this performance because it had been a few years since I had last seen the opera and I knew that Markus Stenz, who was to conduct, was a first-rate musician. For the role of Herod, the Cologne Opera had announced the alternative casting of Josef Protschka and Alexander Fedin, though not indicating which performances each would sing. Fedin, a Russian tenor in the Cologne ensemble, tended only to sing minor roles and, I felt, would be overparted as Herod. On the other hand, Protschka had had an international career as a dramatic tenor. He had become Professor at the Cologne Musik Hochschüle and now made only occasional stage appearances, and so I was rather keen to hear him. I therefore sent an email to the Cologne Opera, indicating that I planned to attend a particular Sunday matinee performance of Salome, and inquiring whether Protschka would sing Herod that day. Yes, I was told in the reply, he was due to sing that performance.

You can imagine my rage when, on the Sunday in question, I arrived at the Cologne Opera House only to find the name of Fedin, and not Protschka, on the cast list. Perhaps my judgement was affected, but I did not enjoy the performance, there being insufficient compensation in the conducting of Stenz to compensate for the silly, vulgar production by Katharina Thalbach set in a modern restaurant, and unsurprisingly an ineffective Herod.

Something should be said of the logistics of operatic excursions. I have already referred to a period spent in Strasbourg and of my journeys from there across the Rhine. Others of my professional bases have included Antwerp, Hamburg, Rotterdam and Maastricht. The last of these cities is in Limburg, the southernmost point of the Netherlands and enticingly placed between Flemish Belgium to the west, Francophone Belgium to the south, and Germany to the east. Paradoxically, Amsterdam, the only Dutch city with a permanent opera company, is too far away for a return journey to and from an evening performance. But, by way of compensation, Antwerp and Brussels, both of which have excellent opera companies, are easily reached. Liège is only a short distance away up the river Maas, or Meuse as it becomes when you cross the linguistic frontier, although the quality of what is offered by the Opéra Royal de Wallonie is, shall we say, variable.

Just across the German border is Aachen, a less interesting town than its history (Charlemagne's residence and the place where the old Kings of Germany were crowned) would imply. Also, in my experience, performances at the opera house there are best avoided. However, further to the east is Cologne, while to the north the Deutsche Oper am Rhein performs both at Düsseldorf and Duisburg. The latter lies in the Ruhr basin, a densely populated and once heavily industrialised region of Germany. The region is by no means a tourist's paradise, though the major cities are not as ugly as is often assumed, and they contain some important art museums as well as interesting buildings, including—as I pointed out in Chapter Two—Aalto's beautiful opera house in Essen. A number of the Ruhr cities proudly maintain their own opera companies: in addition to Essen, Gelsenkirchen, Dortmund, Wuppertal and Hagen. An attempt made in the 1990s to merge the Gelsenkirchen and Wuppertal companies proved to be so unpopular, that the decision had to be reversed. The contrast with Britain, where one company, Opera North, has to serve all of the towns in industrial Yorkshire and Lancashire, as well as Newcastle and Nottingham, could not be greater.

In my younger days, I would invariably travel by car for my operatic excursions in this part of Germany, a practice which created a challenge for my navigational skills. Finding one's way into and out of foreign cities is not easy, particularly after nightfall, and I recall one unhappy experience, when driving away from a performance of *Boris Godunov* in Krefeld, I found the wheels of my car stuck in a sideway of tramway tracks, having lost my way from the road.

The appearance of "satnavs" changed all of this. In October 2007, just a day before my departure for Maastricht, my brother-in-law demonstrated to me how they worked, and I was so convinced of their likely utility that I rushed to buy one so that I might take it with me. Predictably, "Mrs Tom Tom", as I call her (I prefer being instructed by a female, rather than a male, voice), proved to be a godsend, guiding me that autumn without difficulty to and from opera houses in places like Bonn, Brussels (that city is otherwise a driver's nightmare), Cologne, and Mönchengladbach.

Driving is, however, tiring, even with a satnav and, as I have grow older, I have increasingly preferred railway travel. Now although it is very relaxing to sit in trains, they do not always take you exactly where and when you want to go. Between Maastricht and the German opera houses is problematic because rail connections across national borders are not good. I therefore developed a park-and-ride solution. I drove across the border to a small town with a station, close to the autobahn for easy access, and with ample parking facilities. My favourite stations were Eschweiler, between Aachen and Cologne, and Herzogenrath, between Aachen and Düsseldorf.

As regards timing, the key was to know when the last train back to, say, Eschweiler or Herzogenrath would leave from the station near the opera house I was attending. As my experience in Mainz described at the beginning of this chapter reveals, this then has to be related to the likely duration of the performance, and the time taken to get on foot, or sometimes by taxi, if you can find one, from the theatre to that station. Although such calculations might suggest the high probability of catching the last train, it has to be recognised that opera performances do not always run to time.

Of course, it is always possible to leave the theatre before the curtain comes down, but normally you will not wish to do this and, in any case, it is somewhat difficult and embarrassing when you are in the middle of a row. For that reason, I try to find a seat near an exit if I think that there is a serious risk of having to make an early departure. Even then, during the last act, you may have to glance occasionally at your watch to see how close it is getting to the deadline you have set for leaving—not always easy, especially in an auditorium with dimmed lighting. In any case, it does not facilitate emotional involvement in a work if you are worrying about getting away and you feel yourself thinking that, for example, Isolde and her conductor are taking too long over the *Liebestod*. Such be the trials and tribulations of opera excursions.

CHAPTER FOUR

SICKNESS, STRIKES AND OTHER CALAMITIES

It was July 2005 and I had taken my place in the Staatstheater at Saarbrücken and was looking forward to a performance of Smetana's *Dalibor*, a work which is rarely given outside the Czech Republic, but which is a fine, heroic piece in the mould of Beethoven's *Fidelio*. Moreover, for a relatively small company, Saarbrücken had assembled an interesting cast, including, in the title role, the Austrian tenor Rudolf Schasching, who was about to join the Zürich Opera, and, as the heroine Milada, Jayne Casselman, an American soprano who had gained a reputation in Germany in Wagnerian roles. While we were waiting for the conductor, there was a movement from behind the curtains and the theatre administrator appeared. A communal groan circulated around the auditorium: opera audiences know that this means bad news. The only question is: how bad?

We were told that Jayne Casselman was sick but it had been possible to find a replacement, Wilja Ernst-Mosuraitis, a Lithuanian based in Karlsruhe. She had performed the role of Milada there, but not for a year or so; and, in any event she was unfamiliar with the production. So she would sing from a lectern at the side of the stage, while the part would be acted by the assistant director, Annette Radenheimer. This is by no means an unusual solution, but in general the indisposed singer does the acting, because he or she can more convincingly open the mouth as if singing, which increases dramatic plausibility. Perhaps Miss Casselman was too ill to do this; or perhaps as a "guest" of the company, it was thought unreasonable to ask her. In any event, the performance, with this handicap, got underway and on the whole went well.

The first scene of Act Two of the opera takes place in a street below the castle in which Dalibor is imprisoned. The decor, by Herbert Schaefer, was very striking: a snow covered slope winding up the stage was surrounded by, on one side, a huge brick wall and, on the other, a metal structure. As the curtain came down, the music ended on an optimistic note as we learned of plans to set Dalibor free. Then we waited for the curtain to go up on the next scene, which was to take place in the gaoler's house. But nothing happened. After five minutes, there was rustling behind the curtains and the administrator appeared again. It was an evening of misfortune, he told us. Now the machinery which was to move the scenery had got stuck and the rest of the performance would have to be played with the setting of Act Two, Scene One. In truth, that did create a problem, because the gaoler's house and subsequently Dalibor's dungeon had to have the snowy slope as their central feature. But one admired the efforts of the performers to overcome this second setback. The show must go on.

I have the impression that opera is more vulnerable to things going wrong than any other of the performing arts. Why should this be? Most obviously minor ailments, particularly colds, can more seriously affect a singer's ability to deliver than that of, say, an actor or an orchestral musician. Might it also have something to do with the emotional pressure generated by the combination of drama and music? Two famous conductors, Felix Mottl and Joseph Keilberth, both died during performances of *Tristan und Isolde* and strangely in the same opera house at Munich. Well, you may say, conducting *Tristan* is an ideal way to leave this world; on the other hand I cannot imagine that it has since been easy to engage conductors for this work in Munich.

Happily, I have not been present at any fatalities in the opera house, though in Koblenz, in 2009, I was present when a young Korean bass, Jongmin Lim, collapsed while singing the title role in the last Act of Massenet's *Don Quichotte*. Ironically this occurred during Don Quixote's death scene when, in a delirium, he sees and hears Dulcinea. So it did not seem to me that there was anything untoward, until the other performers on the stage rushed to his aid in a way which was not entirely in keeping with their roles, and the curtain suddenly came down. As I left the theatre, after the premature ending to the opera, an ambulance was taking the singer to hospital. His condition cannot have been too serious because it is pleasant to report that within a few weeks he was back performing on the stage.

Then there is the strange fact that several opera houses have been afflicted by fire in recent times. I have already related in Chapter Two how Venice's La Fenice was destroyed in 1996. This was only two years after the same thing had happened to the almost equally famous Liceu opera house in Barcelona. In 1987 the Frankfurt Oper was very badly damaged, the suspected arsonist being an East German refugee; and in 2009 there was a serious fire at the construction site of a high-profile new opera house in Guangzhou, China. In December 1975 I saw a production of *Fidelio* at the Hamburg Staatsoper, but without the decor for the First Act, since that had been destroyed in a fire at the theatre warehouse a month previously. Nor should we forget the destruction of the Maltings in Snape on the first night of the Aldeburgh Festival in 1969.

Emotional pressure can hardly account for these happenings. If they result from arson, then the fact that opera houses are regarded as symbols of power and wealth may have something to do with it. Otherwise, we are left with the possibility of some mysterious divine intervention, responding to the notorious suggestion of Pierre Boulez, that opera houses should be burned down.

In May 2008 I was present at a performance of Gounod's *Roméo et Juliette*, given by Opera North at the Leeds Grand Theatre. We were only a little way into Act One, and the young Slovenian soprano Bernarda Bobro, making her British debut as Juliet, had just finished her famous waltz aria, *"Je veux vivre"*, when the safety curtain descended and the fire alarm sounded. We quickly evacuated the theatre and waited outside for further news, and I remember thinking, first Barcelona, then Venice, now Leeds. But the worst did not happen. The alarm was a result of a technical defect and after twenty minutes or so we were allowed to resume our seats. As a reward for our patience, Miss Bobro sang the waltz aria again and this jolliest of tunes seemed an appropriate celebration for escaping the fate of those other opera houses.

An opera excursionist's worst nightmare is to arrive at the theatre, perhaps after a long journey, only to see the sign "Performance Cancelled". It has happened to me on far too many occasions for my general state of health and happiness. The main cause is the indisposition of a singer and the failure to have available, or to find, a replacement. Of course, the management will try to come up with a solution to the problem, since cancellation is costly in all sorts of ways. The major opera houses, and in some countries including Britain even the provincial companies, have a system of reserves to cover the principal roles. These singers may be familiar with the production, as well as the work, and substitution can easily be undertaken.

By making a strong impression when standing-in for more famous artists, younger singers can quickly establish a reputation, thus giving a kick-start to their international career. In September 2002 I had purchased a ticket for *Ariadne auf Naxos* at Covent Garden, but was most disappointed when I learned that Natalie Dessay, who had been scheduled for the role of Zerbinetta, had pulled out. I knew nothing of her replacement, a young German soprano, Marlis Petersen, but she gave an outstanding performance which led to other major international engagements. Strangely, the situation was almost to repeat itself in 2010. *Hamlet* by Ambroise Thomas was to get its first performance at the New York Met for 103 years, with Dessay as Ophelia. Ten days before the opening night, Dessay fell sick and cancelled. Petersen was invited from Vienna, learned the part in six days, and saved the show.

Sometimes, though not often, you can be lucky in that the replacement produces a higher-quality performance than might have been given by the singer originally cast in the role. For the Empress in *Die Frau ohne Schatten* which I saw at Mannheim in 1973, Enriquetta Tarres from Stuttgart stepped in at short notice for an indisposed Eva Maria Molnar. During the interval I recall overhearing one member of the audience say to another, "Das war ein Glück" ("that was a piece of luck"), implying that she had not had high expectations of Frau Molnar. And in Essen, in 1993, I was not too disappointed when, as Gurnemanz in *Parsifal,* the competent but unexciting Harald Stamm had to be replaced, and the management were able to acquire from Vienna one of the leading Wagnerian basses of the day, Kurt Rydl.

Strangely, Rydl was involved in another of my replacement experiences, but this time he was the ailing singer. The occasion was an eagerly awaited performance of *Der Rosenkavalier* in Amsterdam in May 2011. When I booked my tickets a few months earlier, the cast list was, indeed, enticing: Simon Rattle was to conduct, and his wife Magdalena Kožená was to join Anne Schwanewilms and Rydl in the leading roles. Before the series of performances had begun, Kožená had cancelled—the second time she had done this to me. Then, before the curtain went up, an announcement was made that Kurt Rydl had a throat infection. He would act the part on the stage but Ochs would be sung from the wings by Rúni Brattaberg, a bass hailing from the Faroe Islands. He was scheduled to play the small part of the Police Commissar in Act Three, and we were left wondering what would happen, as there is a confrontation between Ochs and the Commissar at that point in the opera.

From his lectern, at the side of the stage, Brattaberg did a fine job in his vocal characterisation of the coarse and lecherous nobleman during the first two Acts. Then, in Act Three, when there was a cry of *"Polizei"*, he charged, now appropriately costumed, onto the stage and was entirely convincing as the representative of officialdom. But clearly he could not sing Ochs as well and fortunately Rydl was able to growl his way through several bars during their encounter.

Many replacement singers, particularly those not engaged to cover roles and who have been summoned at relatively short notice, will be unfamiliar with the production. In my earlier opera-going days, when the majority of productions were in a traditional style, that was not a significant handicap, although there might be a delay in getting the performance underway as the singer had to be shown movements around the stage. However, in more recent times, the huge diversity in dramatic interpretations and production styles has made it much more difficult for late replacements to fit into a particular presentation, and the solution adopted in Amsterdam of singing from the side, or pit, with someone else acting the role, is encountered much more frequently.

There have been other examples of ingenuity and enterprise in dealing with illness. In 1995 I was in Bolton for an attractive double bill of Chabrier's *Une éducation manquée* and Donizetti's *Il campanello di notte* given by a local opera group called Opera 74. It must be a real headache for amateur and semi-professional companies, operating on a shoestring budget, to cope with illness. When the bass who had the leading role in the Donizetti could not sing, it looked as if the performance would have to be abandoned. However, happily someone in the company knew David Owen Lewis, a veteran of the Opera North Chorus, and a very good singer-actor. Although he had never encountered the part before, he gamely agreed to take it on and to do so, not from the side, but on stage, acting as well as singing, all the time holding and reading the score. Admittedly the role of Don Annibale Pistacchio is a rather stock one—an old husband whose wedding night with his young bride is constantly interrupted by her erstwhile lover ringing the door bell. But one could only marvel at the ability of Owen Lewis to perform it so successfully from scratch.

Another unusual solution occurred at the Théâtre de la Monnaie in Brussels during the run of Cavalli's baroque opera *La Calisto* in 1993. The audience was not allowed into the auditorium when the performance was due to begin but had to wait three-quarters of an hour before it was told what was happening. One of the mezzo-sopranos, Monica Bacelli, was unable to sing and a replacement could not be found. The performance would nevertheless take place. Her solo arias would be cut but her contributions to duets and parts of her recitative would be sung by the conductor (no less!) from the pit. No, we did not have a female conductor that evening. Rather, it was the famous counter-tenor René Jacobs, who could encompass the mezzo-soprano range without difficulty.

It was a strange but wonderful experience, not the least because of the beautiful production and designs by Herbert Wernicke. I enjoyed the evening so much that when, three years later, I was in Belgium and found that *La Calisto* was being revived, I went to see it again, with Maestro Jacobs conducting but not singing. It was another very good performance, but it did not erase the memory of the first evening and of how the overcoming of adversity can add to the impact made by committed artists.

Maybe, like me, you have a yen for catching operatic rarities. In December 1991, I had a meeting in Utrecht on a Friday and, as you will realise, having read Chapter Three, that meant an operatic excursion during the ensuing weekend. The attraction was a real rarity given at Bielefeld: *Die fremde Erde* by Rathaus. When I first saw this announced, I thought that this must mean that the opera was being given at the Town Hall, rather than the City Theatre, because that is the English translation of "Rathaus". But no, Karol Rathaus was a twentieth-century Austrian-Polish composer, one of a number of Central European Jewish composers who wrote some interesting operas in the 1920s and 1930s, only to have their works banned by the Nazis. Others included Franz Schreker, Erich Korngold, Alexander von Zemlinsky and Walter Braunfels. To their credit, some of the German opera companies have been exploring this repertory, reviving works which their predecessors had not been allowed to perform. Hence *Die fremde Erde* in Bielefeld.

But do not expect me to tell you anything more about the opera, because I did not see it. Having travelled four hours by train from

Utrecht, I arrived at the doors of the Bielefeld theatre only to find that, because one of the singers was sick, the performance had been cancelled. Yet the long journey was not entirely wasted, because *Don Giovanni* was performed instead. We had, therefore, not the replacement of a singer, but the replacement of an opera. The *Don Giovanni* was not very good, or perhaps my judgement was coloured by my disappointment at missing the Rathaus piece.

I had a similar experience in 2002 in Kiel where I had a ticket for another of these twentieth-century rarities, *Christophorus* by Schreker, although in this case the replacement was an Offenbach operetta, *Orpheus in the Underworld*. It may seem odd that it is possible to have available, at short notice, all the performers necessary for an alternative piece, but in countries operating the repertory system—see Chapter Three—relatively few of the house ensemble will have engagements elsewhere. Nevertheless I was surprised that when, in November 1998, the performance of Hans Werner Henze's *König Hirsch* at the Komische Oper Berlin was cancelled, it was replaced by *Love of the Three Oranges*. Although this Prokofiev comic opera is far from being a rarity, it is not as familiar as *Don Giovanni* and *Orpheus in the Underworld*, and is a demanding work to mount. All credit, then, to the company for providing its patrons with this solution.

As it happens, a couple of years previously I had missed, through singer illness, another performance at the Komische Oper, this time the exotic Rimsky-Korsakov piece, *The Legend of the Invisible City of Kitezh*. (I have had bad luck with this opera. When the Kirov company gave it at the 1995 Edinburgh Festival I was unable to obtain a ticket.) The replacement this time was *The Magic Flute*. Now when I was in Bielefeld and Kiel, I attended the replacement performances because these are small towns and, frankly, there was not much else to do there. But in Berlin there is an embarrassment of riches, and at the Deutsche Oper, one of the two other opera houses, *Tristan and Isolde* was scheduled for that evening. So rather than see my umpteenth *Magic Flute*, I dumped the ticket and went across town for the Wagner. And this was a good decision. Conducted by the excellent Christian Thielemann, in an elderly but still very effective production by Götz Friedrich, and with two of the leading Wagnerian singers at the peak of their form, Gabriele Schnaut and René Kollo, this was an outstanding *Tristan*. It made me realise that not all cancellations are calamitous.

So you have planned an operatic excursion and the possibility of a performance being cancelled because of singer illness is worrying you. What are the chances of this happening? Well, in these days, when you are supposed to undertake a health and safety risk assessment for nearly everything, including a whist drive at the village hall, perhaps you should do something similar. What information will you need for this purpose?

On the basis of my experience, the risk of a performance being cancelled is about one in a hundred, but there are several factors which might increase, or reduce, this figure. First and foremost, there is the opera which is being given. If it is a popular work and frequently performed, such as *Rigoletto* or *Don Giovanni*, it should be very easy to find a replacement available because there will be many singers with the relevant role in their repertory. If on the other hand, like *Die fremde Erde* or *Christophorus,* it is an obscure piece, very few singers beyond those who have prepared it for your theatre will know the piece; and the question then will be whether someone is willing, perhaps at only a few hours' notice, to sight-read it and sing from the pit or the side of the stage. But sometimes, even with a relatively rare work, you may be lucky. In 2010 I was in Duisburg for *Phaedra*, another opera by Henze which had been mounted by only one other German company, Heidelberg, since its première in Berlin in 2007. When the singer of Aphrodite reported on the morning of a matinee performance that she had a cold, the chances of finding a replacement must have been pretty small, but the management were able to locate Marianne Lichdi who had sung the role in Heidelberg in 2008, and she was flown in.

Secondly, it depends on the country and company where the performance is to be given. As I have indicated, the chance of one of the regular British opera companies cancelling is very low; but if you are in Germany, where there are less systematic arrangements for covering singers, the possibility is greater. Of relevance, also, is geographical location. If the theatre is near an airport with good connections, the chance of getting a replacement from a distance is higher than if it is rather remote. My evidence for this comes from an unhappy experience in Oldenburg. This is a town in the western part of Lower Saxony, at some distance from a major urban area. In a period of four weeks in November 2008, two performances for which I had tickets at the theatre there were cancelled, first Beethoven's *Fidelio,* then three weeks later the Cavalli opera *Giustino.* As you can imagine, I was exasperated, and particularly with the *Fidelio* cancellation, not only because I had already travelled to Oldenburg from Hamburg for that performance, but also because the opera is so frequently performed in Germany that I could not understand why a replacement singer could not be found. So I wrote to the Intendant to complain. In his reply he informed me that Oldenburg is badly placed for transport and that the singer's illness occurred too late to get a replacement from the nearest airport.

Once you have undertaken your risk assessment, what steps should you take to deal with the risk, particularly if the operatic excursion involves some travel? My strategy is as follows. In the days before the performance or performances, I keep an eye on the websites of the theatres which I intend to visit, to make sure that the performance is still scheduled. Then, if the piece is a rarity and is to be given in Germany, I telephone the theatre box office before I set out with the question, *"Es läuft heute Abend?"* (Is it on this evening?). However, that is not always possible. In October 2006, I had a ticket for *La Cifra* by Salieri to be given in Cologne in apparently the work's first revival in modern times. So, this was definitely a risky venture from Maastricht, where I was based fifty-five miles away. Unfortunately the performance was on a Sunday and the box office was not open until an hour before curtain up. That meant that even if I had called en route from a mobile telephone—which I did not—I would not have been far from Cologne before obtaining reliable information. And yes, the worst did happen, for when I arrived, there was that awful notice on the theatre door, that due to a singer's illness, *"die Vorstellung fällt ab"*.

I also attempt to devise a contingency plan, searching for a relatively attractive alternative, should the risk of cancellation materialise. This might be a concert or a play in the town where the performance is to take place, or an opera in a nearby town, assuming that I can get there in time. So, when I set off for the Sunday matinee performance of Henze's *Phaedra*, I knew that if this was cancelled I could get to see Poulenc's *Dialogues des Carmelites* which was to be given at the same time in Düsseldorf, only fifteen minutes from Duisburg by train.

If the contingency plan is to be put into effect, you must know of the cancellation as soon as possible. In consequence, as soon as I arrive at my destination, I rush to the theatre to see whether or not a cancellation notice has been posted. If there is no such notice, I can then check in at a hotel or go to a restaurant for a meal, or whatever, but I do not fully relax until, seated in the theatre, I see the conductor raise the baton ...

The illness of a singer is not the only reason why a performance may be cancelled. At the Edinburgh Festival in 1966, I was at the King's Theatre for *Wozzeck*, given by the Stuttgart Opera. The orchestra had already tuned up when an announcement was made that, due to the sudden indisposition of the conductor, Carlos Kleiber, the performance would not take place. This must be a rare occurrence, because, with a short period of notice, almost certainly an assistant conductor or other member of the musical staff of the company will be available to take over.

Technical difficulties, as they are sometimes euphemistically referred to, can also intervene. In February 1993 I had driven from Antwerp to Eindhoven to see a touring production of Verdi's rarely performed *Stiffelio*. A problem had arisen in transferring the set from the previous venue and the opera had to be given in concert form. Some concert performances can be very good, but I was not expecting this and, particularly after my long journey, I felt cheated.

Weather conditions must be very severe to affect ordinary opera performances, preventing you or the performers from getting to the theatre. (I do remember a late start to *Don Carlos* in Duisburg, because we had to wait forty minutes for the Russian baritone who was to sing Rodrigo to arrive. He had got stuck in a train somewhere near Düsseldorf though this was not due to weather). But it is of course a significant hazard for open-air performances, of which there are quite a few during the summer festival season.

Cricket lovers in Britain are very accustomed to matches being cancelled or abandoned. As an operamaniac, I am not so stoical. At the Munich Festival in 1987, I was in the Alter Hof for *Die Benauerin* by Carl Orff, a play with music, rather than an opera. But it lasted only thirty minutes before the rain came down and the performance was abandoned. Since those thirty minutes had been much more play than music, I acquired little idea as to the work's idiom and stomped away in the wet.

Presumably the weather in Verona is reasonably reliable because at the Arena there is no "singing in the rain". But spectators at other open-air venues are more generously treated. The first such event I attended was at Koblenz in 1964, a performance of *The Merry Widow* being given on a stage erected on the Rhine. It poured; while we huddled under umbrellas, the singers bravely carried on, having donned transparent rainproof covers for their costumes. However, the more typical solution is to transfer the performance to an indoor venue. The problem with this is that the number of spectators in an open-air arena is often too large to be accommodated within a theatre and some alternative building has to be used. This was the fate of the performance of Verdi's *Attila* at the Antikenfestspiele at Trier in 2005. It should have taken place in the wonderful Roman ruins in that city, and the sports arena to which it was transferred completely lacked the appropriate atmosphere.

Industrial action is a more serious matter than weather, and can have a devastating effect, if for no other reason than that it may be part of the trade union strategy not to give much advance notice of a strike. This happened when I was in Paris in 2000. I was to take my sister-in-law Hélène to Prokofiev's *War and Peace*, a performance which I was eagerly anticipating because I had seen the opera only once previously and the Opéra Bastille had promised a fine cast, including several famous Russian singers. With the known strength of the French public sector unions, Parisians are relatively accustomed to disruptions of this kind. But when, an hour before the performance was to begin, I learned of the cancellation, I was furious and left the theatre in a huff.

I should have stayed calm and gone immediately to the box office to get my money back, because it took nine months for the theatre to respond to my written request for a refund, another source of grievance. Hélène and I had to make a quick decision as to what to do, and, to add salt to the wound, we made a bad choice. We opted for the play *La Dame aux Camélias*, the source of Verdi's *La Traviata*, in the original Alexandre Dumas version. Perhaps we had been attracted by the prospect of seeing Isabelle Adjani, a well-known film actress, in the title role, but the production was old-fashioned and stilted. A bad evening, indeed.

I was more sanguine when, later in that season, a visit to the company's *Lucia di Lammermoor* suffered the same fate as *War and Peace*. *Lucia* is a sufficiently familiar work for one lost performance not to be a considered a disaster. In any event, I queued up for my refund and then resorted to my contingency plan, a Goldoni play, *Barouf à Chioggio*, presented at a fringe theatre on the Left Bank: it was superb.

Of course, industrial action is not unknown in Britain. In 1991 there was a dispute between the Musicians Union and the Royal Opera House, resulting in the cancellation of the first few performances of a rare revival of *Les Huguenots* by Meyerbeer. I had not then seen this work which was the backbone of the repertory at Covent Garden in the second half of the nineteenth century. So I was bitterly disappointed to be deprived of it, even though the production by John Dew was roundly condemned by the critics when it was eventually given.

In the autumn of 1977 I had a ticket for a performance at Covent

Garden of *Don Carlos,* perhaps my favourite Verdi opera. Unfortunately, it was during a period when there was another dispute between the orchestra and the management. On this occasion, it had not given rise to a strike; rather the members of the orchestra indicated that they would "work to rule". In the 1970s it was quite common for industrial action to take this form, and it would generally involve employees, such as those working in public transport, "going slow", so that a bus journey would, for example, take twice as long as usual.

Now you can see the dangers if musicians were to "work to rule" in this way: presumably every *allegro* would be performed as an *andante*. That did not happen at the performance of *Don Carlos*. Rather, "working to rule" meant that the orchestra would not play after ten o'clock in the evening. *Don Carlos* is a long opera, playing to almost five hours if uncut. So, out went the First Act, the Fontainebleau scene; so also portions of Acts Three and Four, resulting in, as I recall, some untidy improvisation in the production. When it came to Act Five, and the great last duet of Carlos and Elisabeth, ten o'clock was fast approaching; and was it just my impression, or was the conductor Miguel Gomez-Martinez hurrying the singers along, in order to finish on time?

CHAPTER FIVE

TICKETS

At the Munich Festival in the summer of 1977 my need for tickets could not have been greater. There was a performance of the Richard Strauss opera *Die Frau ohne Schatten* bringing together two of the greatest singers of the post-war generation, Birgit Nilsson and Dietrich Fischer-Dieskau. My girlfriend, Catherine, was visiting from Strasbourg, four hours away by train, and she was in love with Fischer-Dieskau. Unfortunately, all seats had been sold months previously.

A colleague had advised me to go to the most expensive hotel in town, Die Vierjahrzeiten, and ask the head porter if he could sell me a ticket. I did so. "Ah, yes," he said when I told him what I wanted, "that's a performance with Birgit Nilsson, isn't it?" He then opened his desk drawer, revealing a quantity of apparently unobtainable tickets. Without a blush, he offered me two seats for 100 Marks each. Although I saw that the original price of each ticket was 30 Marks, I accepted without hesitation and later was to feel that the money was very well spent. It was the last time I was to hear Nilsson live. She was nearly sixty, but vocally she was still extraordinary, the sound of her soprano soaring above the big Strauss orchestra, and with that very personal "heft" which gave emotional depth and colour to what she was singing. And I recall vividly that when the two great singers appeared together to take their bow, Fischer-Dieskau—whose own performance had been itself very impressive—with a typical courteous gesture deferred to her, as if to say, "She deserves your ovation; I can't match her".

Ten years later we were in Dresden and of course wanted to attend performances at the famous, and beautiful, Semperoper. Arriving at the box office, I was informed that there were no tickets left. At first dismayed, I then recalled my strategy at Munich. Would a black market transaction which had been so easy in capitalist Western Germany be possible in the socialist German Democratic Republic? The East German regime was known to be rigid and, in any event, was not hospitable to Western tourists. I was therefore nervous as I crossed the river Elbe and walked up to the main hotel frequented by foreigners. But the porter there treated my request as if it were routine, and supplied my needs with an equivalent mark-up to that gained by his Munich equivalent. I am still unclear whether or not this was legal, and whether he, and I, had taken a risk of arrest and imprisonment.

What the Munich and Dresden episodes illustrate is that true opera enthusiasts cannot bear the idea of missing a performance that they passionately want to see and will find the means, fair or foul, of securing a ticket. In the economics textbooks there is a technical expression to describe this type of behaviour: it is called "inelastic demand". In relation to most goods which people buy, an increase in price reduces the amount which they are prepared to pay for—demand is "elastic"— but when the desire for the particular goods is very high, price increases do not change the amount buyers wish to purchase, or only to a small degree. When introducing this concept to my students, I have generally given the example of my own opera-going behaviour.

So, with the "inelasticity" of my demand for opera performances, is there no limit to what I am prepared to pay? Of course there is, and, in any event, it depends on the performance in question. A good illustration of this comes from my student days when I often used to try to get a ticket to stand at the back of the Stalls Circle at Covent Garden. In Chapter Two I described the excellent system at the Vienna Staatsoper, where you can get a *Stehplatz* at any performance. The arrangements at Covent Garden were very different. Standing tickets would only be available a couple of hours before the performance, and then only if all seats in the house had been sold. It was therefore often a gamble, foregoing the purchase of a cheaper seat at the top of the house, in the hope that everything would be sold and you could get a standing ticket by queuing on the day.

Between us enthusiasts in the queue (they included Brian McMaster and Nicholas Payne, later to become well-known administrators of opera companies) and the box office manager, there was often a game of bluff and counter-bluff. Our strategy was based on the assumption that he would know that most of us could not afford a seat in the more expensive parts of the house and that he would make more money if he were to sell the standing tickets even though some seats were still unsold. Sometimes he would do this, but if he was shrewd he would realise that the desire of some of us to attend a particular performance was so great, that in the end we would yield and scrape up enough money for an expensive seat.

This is what happened to me in 1967. I travelled from Oxford to London to see *Arabella*, another work by Richard Strauss, in the Royal Opera House's first production of that work, conducted by Solti and sung by, among others, Joan Carlyle and (again) Dietrich Fischer-Dieskau. Obviously a very special performance, but when I arrived in the queue, I was horrified to discover that, contrary to my expectations, quite a few seats remained unsold, and all my efforts to convince the box office manager that I only had enough money for a standing ticket failed. So, rather than face travelling back to Oxford with the frustration of missing the performance, and after considerable soul-searching, I coughed up £4 for a seat in the Stalls, a huge amount for me in those days.

As I grew older, so the resources I had available to buy opera tickets— though never great—increased. At Covent Garden, for example, in the 1980s and 1990s, I allowed myself to be elevated from the Amphitheatre (or the standing area) to the Balcony Stalls and sometimes even the Stalls.

Unfortunately, in more recent times, the price of tickets, especially for expensive productions with top-class performers, seems to have gone up faster than my income—for the better seats, it may be in the range of £150–£200. There has to be something special about a performance for me to be willing to pay over £100 for a ticket. So, on my occasional visits to the Royal Opera House, I now often find myself back in the Amphitheatre, reliving my younger days.

The cost of opera tickets varies enormously between different countries. To some extent this may be a question of relative prosperity which is reflected in the exchange rate so that, for example, opera-going in Eastern Europe was, and still is, very cheap—you can get a good seat in some houses for £10–£15. But, in the West, the most important factor is the level of public subsidy. In the UK, public funding accounts for around twenty-five to thirty per cent of the income of the major opera companies; in France, Germany and Italy, the equivalent figure is some seventy-five to eighty per cent. This means that tickets in these countries can be relatively inexpensive by British standards. In Germany, for example, at major theatres such as Cologne, Hamburg or Stuttgart, you can still get a decent seat for most performances for under €50; and at smaller theatres tickets are still remarkably cheap. In November 2011, I was in the lovely town of Görlitz, on the German-Polish border, and paid only €21 for a place in the centre of the fifth row of the stalls. The quality of what I saw and heard was, incidentally, excellent.

Where, as in the Anglo-Saxon countries, public subsidy is not so generous, some of the difference may be made up by private sponsorship. British opera companies have striven hard on this front and with some success, but the level of support is nowhere near that secured by their American equivalents whose seat prices therefore compare favourably with our own. You might think that this is a very modern problem, but it is not. When Handel operas were being performed at the Royal Academy in London in the 1720s and 1730s, the income from ticket sales (10s 6d for a stall, 5s for the gallery, probably around £100 and £45 respectively in today's values) was insufficient to meet costs and £1000 per season from the royal purse, as well as contributions from other sources, had to be made available.

Could the sums demanded for individual seats have been increased? Maybe, but in Handel's day, as in our own, prices must reflect what people are willing to pay. Typically those charged for elite opera festivals, such as Salzburg, Bayreuth, Aix-en-Provence and Glyndebourne are very high. Now my own experience has been that performances at these festivals are often (though not always) outstandingly good. If so, patrons get a decent return for the money they have spent. In any event, I suspect that most of them would recognise that they are paying a premium for the occasion, for the glamour and prestige associated with such performances, and there is no harm in that.

I have greater doubts about the cost of seats at the top international houses, such as La Scala, the Met, Covent Garden, Paris and Vienna. A key factor is that one can there hear the top opera singers currently active, and for many people this is perhaps the most important attraction. Indeed, for very famous singers, some theatres will charge premium prices, knowing that they will have no difficulty in selling all the seats. What happens, then, if the superstar cancels and has to be replaced by a lesser mortal? You might have thought that this is a risk that you take when you buy the ticket, but Covent Garden has exceptionally offered some refund. This was done when, in 1965, Maria Callas was replaced by Marie Collier and, some years later, Pavarotti by Giacomo Aragall. Now Collier and Aragall were both fine artists and it must have been rather galling for them to have been treated as second-rate goods.

Of course, as I shall make clear in Chapter Eight, hearing a great singer live can be a thrilling experience, particularly if the artist combines dramatic with vocal skills. However, the existence of "big names" in a cast does not guarantee an experience of this kind. The singer in question may not be in good form or may not be well suited to the work to be performed. Most important of all, the production may lack dramatic impact, perhaps because it has been in the repertory for a long time and used mainly as a vehicle for jet-setting opera stars. So, if

I had to rate spending, say, £40 on a ticket for a good production given by provincial company without star singers against £100 for famous singers in an international house, but in a nondescript production, I would consider the first of these to be better value.

One ancillary cost of opera-going should not be overlooked, that of buying a programme, particularly if you are like me and wish to keep it as a souvenir. With just a few exceptions—where the supply at the theatre had run out, or where I had mislaid my purchase—I have programmes of all the performances I have attended. My collection therefore takes up a large amount of space on my bookshelves. During the early 1960s, a Covent Garden programme cost one shilling and it was a modest affair, containing simply the cast list, a synopsis of the plot and perhaps a historical note about performances of the work at that theatre. Surprisingly, biographies of the artists did not regularly appear until 1969. Occasionally, and particularly in the case of new or unusual works, there might have been a short introduction to the piece.

Compare that with what you get today. In most of the major houses, programme enthusiasts have to buy what amounts to a book, containing a whole range of material. Sometimes this includes the libretto with a translation, though generally I do not want this and object to it being forced on me. More interesting are the commentaries on the composer, the work and its historical context. You may even find that the conductor and/or stage director contribute an article giving their opinion of the opera and how it should be interpreted. This can be a godsend when what you see on the stage bears little resemblance to the synopsis of the plot which you have also read (see further Chapter Nine). Then there may be extracts from literature and learned writings, photographs and other miscellanea which seem to have only marginal relevance to what you are about to see, and which are obviously "padding". Whether it is worth the £7–£8 or €10 which is typically charged is a moot point.

Before the days of the Internet, booking tickets for opera abroad was a real headache. Festivals might have an application form which had to be sent months in advance. For ordinary performances in foreign theatres, you could send requests by mail, but this was slow and awkward as regards choice of seats and alternative dates. Better by far was to use the telephone, although that was expensive, particularly if you were kept waiting in a queue, and then there might be language difficulties. Another possibility was to purchase through a specialist agency. While this might avoid hassle and problems of communication, it could be expensive and, in my experience, was not always reliable.

In Chapter Two I have described how I paid an agency €60 for a ticket to a performance at La Fenice in Venice and ended up with quite the worst seat I have ever had in an opera house. In 1976 another calamity occurred. Through a German agency, I had booked seats for Catherine and myself to attend a performance of Verdi's *Falstaff* at the Munich Festival. I was informed that I should collect the tickets at the theatre box office. When I arrived, I discovered that the agency had not communicated the order to the theatre and seats had not been reserved for me. *Entsetzlich!* This was yet another Fischer-Dieskau performance— you will recall Catherine's passion for him—and almost certainly all seats were sold. They were, although the poor lady behind the grille, who was in no way responsible but who had to face my fury, was able to find two return tickets; and we were saved.

The work was sung in German rather than Italian—at that time the tradition of performances in translation persisted in even the bigger German houses, at least for comic operas. But in other respects the evening was a delight, mainly because the production by Günther Rennert was stylish and witty; and so I was able to abate my anger until I returned home. Then I set to writing a letter of complaint to the German agency. It so happened that a few years earlier I had published a book on the assessment of compensation for legal wrongs, including two chapters on breach of contract. Using all the best legal jargon I could muster, I told the agency that in addition to reimbursing me for the cost of the tickets which never materialised, they were obliged to pay me for the wasted postal and other costs of my bookings, as well as £50 damages for the non-financial loss of disappointment in not being able to attend a special performance. I did not tell them that I had been able to obtain alternative tickets. After a short delay, I was sent a cheque for all that I had claimed.

Tickets for some venues are notoriously difficult to obtain. Friends and acquaintances are often amazed when I tell them that I have made six visits to the Bayreuth Festival, attending there nineteen performances; they want to know how I managed to get the tickets. The answer is simple. From my first visit in 1967 to 2009, I sent in an application form every year and the ballot system is apparently such that the more frequently one applies unsuccessfully, the greater the chance in a future year of securing what one wants. In any event, my success rate works out at approximately one in seven, which is not extraordinarily high.

Why did I stop applying in 2009? In that year, the artistic directorship of the festival was taken over by Richard Wagner's two great-granddaughters, Eva Wagner-Pasquier and Katharina Wagner. In 2008, I had seen Katharina's production of *Rienzi* in Bremen. It was unbelievably awful: see Chapter Nine. From what I have read, her production of *Die Meistersinger* for the festival was equally bad. I will not return to Bayreuth while she is at the helm.

Tickets for performances at the major provincial opera houses in France and Italy are not always easy for foreigners to obtain. This is because a high proportion of the seats are bought as part of a subscription for the whole season. In my earlier opera-going days I was unaware of this and in 1978, during an Easter break in Italy, turned up at the Bologna opera house, anticipating no problem in getting into a matinee performance of Stravinsky's *The Rake's Progress*, which is by no means a popular work. I was very surprised to learn that all tickets were sold. However, a number of returned tickets became available and, during the (not very good) performance, I noticed that there were quite a few empty seats.

The prospect of finding a return ticket when most have been purchased by way of subscription is therefore good, and if, as in the Bologna case, you are already in the town, it is well worth trying. But if you have to travel some distance to the opera house, you might hesitate, not wanting to risk a fruitless journey. When in Bayreuth in the 1990s, I happened to get into conversation with a young Englishman who had travelled there, and was staying for a week or so. He had no ticket, but queued for each performance for a few hours in the hope of getting a return. He had not yet succeeded, but still had a few days to go. Although I have known some bad cases of Wagnermania, that seemed to me to be nothing but insanity.

In 1985 I was staying with friends at Viareggio, a seaside resort in Northern Tuscany. I discovered that Giordano's *Andrea Chenier* was being performed at Lucca, an attractive walled town not far away, but still involving an hour or so on the bus. Again, all the seats had been sold for the *stagione lirica*—perhaps not so surprising because *Andrea Chenier* is a popular *verismo* opera and some well-known singers had been engaged.

My host Adriano took the matter into his own hands. He told me not to worry, that he would get a ticket for me. As far as I knew, he had no connections with the world of opera, but he had a little business in Florence importing artefacts. He telephoned the Lucca theatre, informing them that he was a member of the Florence Fine Arts Association, or something similar, and that he would like a ticket for *Andrea Chenier* for an English colleague, il Dottore Ogus. I arrived at the theatre, still not really believing that this ruse would succeed, but there was indeed a complimentary ticket awaiting me at the box office—and the seat I was given was a very good one. Perhaps there is, after all, some truth in the rumour that the Mafia run some of the Italian opera houses.

Waiting for returns can be a stressful business. This is particularly the case when you are at a foreign, or at least unfamiliar, theatre and you do not know what the conventions are. Do those waiting abide by principles of fairness when queuing? Is the system controlled by the box office staff, so that all returned tickets are channelled through them and they keep a list of names in priority order; or do those with spare tickets negotiate with potential purchasers independently of the box office? If the latter, is it worth your while wandering around, or standing near, the box office with a €50 banknote in your hand, or with a suitable inscribed placard, for example "*Suche Karte*"?

I have waited for returns outside many theatres and in many countries and the overwhelming experience has been that everywhere people obey an implicit code of fairness, based on "first come, first served". More than that, there generally develops a sense of camaraderie, rather than competition, between those waiting, and, if you are foreigner, this can involve very helpful advice. Moreover, I have never come across anyone selling a ticket attempt to exploit the situation and ask for a mark-up on the price—in some countries that may, in any event, be illegal. I have experienced the converse situation where someone has been keen to get rid of a ticket, and, because not all seats have been sold, has offered it at a reduced price (lucky you, if you are a purchaser in this situation).

However much fairness may apply to queuing for a return, that does not help you when you are faced with making an awkward decision. An expensive ticket, outside your normal budget range, turns up twenty minutes before curtain up; should you take it, or wait and hope that a cheaper one may yet become available? And is your answer the same if there are only ten minutes to go? At the other extreme, should you go for a very cheap seat with, say, limited visibility? In making decisions like these, should you be influenced by the number of people ahead of you in the queue who have declined the offer, in the expectation that something better will come along?

Then suppose that there are two of you, and only a single ticket is on offer. Should one of you take it, hoping that another single will eventually turn up? Or should you hold out for what will be either shared misery or shared happiness? At this point, I have an awful confession to make. A few days after Christmas 1990, Catherine and I were in the queue for returns at the Paris Opéra Bastille. The performance in question was *Le Nozze di Figaro*, in the famous Giorgio Strehler production, and with a starry cast: Cecilia Bartoli, Ferrucio Furlanetto, Sergei Leiferkus, Lucia

Popp and Ruth Ann Swenson in the main parts, and veterans Jane Berbié, François Loup and Michel Sénéchal in some of the minor roles. A single ticket came on offer and Catherine insisted that I buy it, her argument being not that it was Christmas, but that my need was greater than hers.

I was convinced that, in her own language, *elle se devouait,* or as we used to say in our family "she made a tomato (i.e. martyr) of herself", but I allowed her to persuade me. And then the performance did not live up to my expectations. This may have been, as I indicated in Chapter Two, because the old Strehler production from the Palais Garnier did not work well in the new, modern theatre. But I suspect that an equally important reason for the disappointment was my sense of guilt.

In the days before the booking of seats by Internet became so easy, I would sometimes risk arriving at a theatre without a ticket, but only of course if I thought that a full house was very unlikely. The advantage of this is that you do not have to commit yourself in advance to being in the town on a particular day and, if there are many empty seats, you can get a feel of the theatre before deciding where you wish to sit. But quite apart from the possibility of the performance being cancelled—which I dealt with in the last chapter—other things can go wrong.

In 1977 I drove from Munich to Nuremberg to see Hans Werner Henze's opera, *Elegy for Young Lovers.* I could not envisage that a contemporary opera like this would attract a big audience; and doubtless I was right. But when I arrived, I discovered that that day it was being given in a *geschlossene Vorstellung;* that is, a performance for a particular group or association and to which members of the public are not admitted. I might have seen the letters "G.V." after the listed performance in the newspaper, but I did not know what they stood for. Unlike a similar experience the previous year in Bratislava (see Chapter Two), I had no local contact to help me find a solution. So I sidled up to the usher who was checking the tickets, explained my ignorance of "G.V." and asked him if he would let me in. His ready compliance with my request was rewarded with twenty Marks.

In the converse situation when you know that there will be a very heavy demand for tickets for a performance, you have to book early, normally on the start date from which tickets become available. In the days before the Internet, the booking could done by post or telephone. If you purchased by post, it was relatively easy to ensure that your letter arrived on or before that date, but it was then a matter outside your control how soon your envelope would be opened. If you used the telephone (and if this was possible on the first day of booking, which was not always the case), you would have to find out the exact time the box office would open, and then dial the appropriate number a few seconds before that time. If you failed then to get through, the line would almost certainly thereafter be engaged, and you would have to dial the number continually until you either succeeded in getting through or you gave up exhausted.

Today, across most of Europe and elsewhere, you can buy opera tickets through the Internet (generally directly from the theatre's own website) and this has made the life of an opera enthusiast so much easier. It does not, however, follow that this method of booking seats is entirely without stress and strain. On one occasion, I found that by mistake—I am not sure if it was mine or that of the website system— I had purchased two tickets for a performance at Antwerp, instead of one. And it needed the exchange of several emails to sort the matter out. But the main problem is when, as with postal and telephone booking, you need to apply for tickets early, before they are all sold.

The theatre website will normally indicate a date and time when booking will open and you must then be online, ready to pounce. The problem is that hundreds of others will be doing the same. With such congestion, the network link will be either very slow or will fail altogether. The booking process involves a number of steps, choosing the performance, the seats, the method of payment and so on. The delay at each stage means that there is a risk that you will be timed out and will have to start the process from the beginning again—and, of course, during all this time, the number of available tickets will be diminishing.

When I applied for tickets for Glyndebourne in 2008, I was over an hour at the computer, having restarted the booking process at least seven or eight times. But my patience was ultimately rewarded and the result was a most enjoyable performance of Monteverdi's *L'Incoronazione di Poppea*, in Robert Carsen's excellent production, conducted by the French baroque specialist, Emmanuelle Haïm, with Alice Coote as Nero and the oh-so-sexy Danielle de Niese as Poppea.

I was a little less fortunate dealing with the Théâtre de la Monnaie in Brussels. In the autumn of 2006 it announced that the tickets for its forthcoming production of *Tristan und Isolde* would come on sale at 12.00 (that is 11.00 British time) on Saturday 23rd September. Now that was very awkward for me because that morning I was travelling by train from London to Oxford, for a reunion dinner at my old college, Magdalen, and would not get to the college before 11.30. Immediately I arrived I asked the college porter where I could find Internet access and he directed to me a café 100 yards away in the High Street. I rushed there.

I had already identified my preferred dates. Several were possible for me, since I would be working in Maastricht, some fifty-five miles away, during the relevant period, but I wished to avoid Tuesday 17th October. On that day Tristan would be sung by Mark Lundberg, clearly a second string to John Keyes, another American tenor, who would sing the role in all the other performances. I had never heard Keyes, but he was the more prominent artist; Lundberg had been a competent Tristan (but no more) in a semi-staged performance that I had attended at the Leeds Town Hall, a year or so previously.

At 11.50, seated in the Internet café, I entered the Monnaie website, but could make only very slow progress getting to what I wanted. I then had the bright idea of switching from the French language section to the Flemish section, because I guessed that the demand for tickets would be higher from the French-speaking community than from the Flemish community. I was right and the system responded much more quickly, but sadly all the decent seats for the performances I wanted were already sold—presumably many of these had been taken up by subscription-holders before general booking had begun. That left only the 17th October and, though I bought a ticket for that day, I have to report that Lundberg was indeed disappointing. If only I had been at home at 11.00 on the Saturday morning!

Let us suppose that you have obtained a ticket for a sold-out performance of a work, production, or with singers, that you have much looked forward to seeing. You stride into the opera house with a keen sense of anticipation. The fact that you pass by some people who are looking for a return may enhance your excitement, not because you get sadistic pleasure from awareness that you have a ticket and they have not, but rather because the heavy demand indicates that others share your expectation of something special. In any event you do not have to worry about securing a seat.

Well, probably not. In November 2007 I had by telephone purchased a ticket for Lehár's operetta, *The Count of Luxemburg*, at the theatre in Mönchengladbach. Arriving twenty minutes before the performance began, I collected the ticket from the box office and went to my seat. It was occupied by an elderly lady. When I politely informed her that she was sitting in my seat, she told me that I must have made a mistake. I showed her my ticket and she showed me hers: it was for the same seat and there had been a double booking.

Knowing from experience that possession is nine-tenths of the law, and realising that the elderly lady was not prepared to move, I went in search of an usherette. She appeared not to believe my story, but, returning with me to the seat, had the evidence in front of her. It was now five minutes before curtain up. She saw a group of empty seats in another row and told me to sit there, so that she could go to the box office to sort the matter out. While she was away, a group of people arrived in the row where I had been placed, and asked me to leave because they had a ticket for my new seat. I was in no position to resist and so had to move again, this time to a seat with relatively poor visibility at the end of a row. I remained undisturbed for the First Act, but the experience had been so perturbing that I found it difficult to concentrate. In any event, I found the Lehár and the production both rather mediocre and decided to leave at the interval.

On my way out, I met the usherette who had been looking for me. She was profuse in her apologies. Apparently the first seat had been sold as part of a subscription and the individual concerned had informed the box office that she could not attend that performance and that they could resell her ticket. Unfortunately, she did not return the ticket to the box office and must have forgotten about her decision to offer it for resale— for she gave it to a friend.

By way of compensation I was offered a complimentary ticket to the next production at the theatre. I declined the offer. Mönchengladbach was not a huge attraction, in terms either of urban landscape or, as I had come to learn, of theatre administration.

CHAPTER SIX

AUDIENCES

In 2010 Helen and I decided to attend the Wexford Festival. We also thought that it would be fun to invite friends to come with us. They readily accepted since not only would Wexford be a new experience for them, but they had never been to Ireland. Then the question arose as to the dress code: what should we wear? I had been to Wexford on three previous occasions, the last time in 1994. I had then worn black tie and I seemed to recall that most of the audience had been similarly attired. But, I thought, that was sixteen years ago and across Europe there had been a movement away from formal dress at opera performances. Also, was not Ireland in a deep financial crisis? Surely, people would not be keen in the circumstances to display wealth. So my recommendation was: let's be smart but not formal.

Boy, did I get it wrong! As we approached the new festival opera house—an impressive replacement of the former cosy but cramped theatre—we noticed some well-dressed people moving in the same direction. It was difficult to ignore the striking contrast between their elegant appearance and the nondescript little terrace houses which surround the theatre. Then, when we entered the foyer, we gaped. It was not simply that in our informal, though smart, outfits, we were in a small minority. It was rather the boldness of the Irish approach which made such an impact; they obviously were taking a huge delight in dressing up for the occasion.

One young lady was dazzling in an all-black attire: elegant long dress, gloves above the elbow, and a rose at the shoulder. Her mother was in a stylish and sophisticated tailored cream suit with a dash of sparkle. Then there was a tall, slim lady with an Edith Sitwell-like appearance, topped with a art-deco headband—fortunately we were not sitting behind her. There were some stunning dresses worn by younger women, but their seniors were not to be outdone, many of them wearing garments of great originality and not a little humour. A woman of mature years was, for example, sporting a handbag in the shape of a motor car. If understandably the men could not display so much variety, they did not lack showmanship. The chap next to me at the cloakroom was depositing a silk top hat and opera cape.

Dress was not the only distinctive feature of the Wexford audience. During the interval my friend dashed to the bar to order some drinks for us. When we joined him, he was obviously enjoying a conversation with an elderly gentleman. I thought that he must have met an old acquaintance and I waited for him to introduce us; but he did not. Later, as we were sipping our wine, he told me that the man was a complete stranger who just struck up a conversation, as they were waiting to be served. By a coincidence—or was it?—when I resumed my seat, my neighbour, another elderly gentleman, asked me if I had enjoyed the First Act; and when I replied that indeed I had, he began to compare the performance with others he had attended that week.

Spontaneous conversation between strangers in a theatre may not be that unusual, but somehow the combination of relishing the occasion, with extravagant, even eccentric, dress, as well as personal cordiality and warmth marked out the Wexford audience as being different from those encountered elsewhere.

Audiences are indeed a fascinating part of the operatic experience. The mere fact of sharing a performance with others adds to its impact. That is one reason why when one is listening or watching at home, a studio recording or filmed production is not the same thing as a live broadcast. Even then, in the comfort of your armchair, you have only a virtual involvement with the people present in the theatre and it cannot compare with physically being there. This is partly because, as I pointed out in Chapter One when discussing live transmissions to cinemas, the presence of the singers makes you aware that they are communicating to, and for, you personally. But it goes beyond this, because the musical and dramatic experience is enhanced by the communal response to it.

That certainly is the case with comic operas since the laughter of others adds something to your own enjoyment of what is funny. Less obviously it also applies to more serious emotions, be they sentimental or tragic. To put this to the test, ask yourself the following hypothetical question: if you had the resources, would you, like King Ludwig II of Bavaria, want a Wagner music drama to be performed for yourself alone? I think that most would answer this in the negative. And then there is the pleasure of joining in applause at the end. Audiences are important.

Audiences vary from one country to another, and also from one type of occasion to another; changes have also occurred over time. Let me start with the question of dress. Traditionally, attending performances in the most prestigious opera houses, such as London's Covent Garden, the Vienna Staatsoper and the New York Met, was associated with wealth and social class, but this did not apply to the "second houses" in these cities—Sadlers Wells, the Volksoper and the New York City Opera. And the distinction was reflected in dress codes, of which there were still some traces when I began my opera-going in the 1960s. Formal attire, in the sense of black dinner jackets and dress shirts for men, long gowns for women, was often to be seen at Covent Garden for regular performances; and the same was true of continental opera houses. But another influence might, by then, have been simply conformism: "dressing up" had become identified with events such as opera, Ascot or Henley. If you went to these, you dressed up even though you were not a member of the upper classes or very wealthy.

With the 1970s and the 1980s came a greater variety of formal wear, for example, tuxedos of different colours and shorter and more exotic gowns, but also, and more importantly, much greater tolerance of informality. Because social conformism has become less important, those who make the effort to dress up may do so with a greater sense of showy glamour. At our first visit to La Fenice in Venice, we were a trifle disappointed that only a small minority of the audience had, like ourselves, decided to go formal. But some of those who did certainly made an impact. In the bar before the performance, I could not keep my eyes off one young lady in an exotic, body-hugging cream lace dress, knee length at the front but with a fishtail touching the floor at the back.

In general, formal attire is now regularly worn only at first nights, gala performances and festivals. Where can one find the best dressed audience? In my experience, the answer would be at the Salzburg Festival, perhaps reflecting the high prices charged for tickets. When we were there in 2001, we encountered innumerable designer outfits which must have cost thousands of pounds—and that does not include the jewellery which came with them. Particularly striking were two elderly ladies, at different ends of the barometer of good taste. One was the epitome of elegance, in a black asymmetric, deconstructed gown with wonderful pointed black lace evening shoes. The other was in a pale blue lace concoction, floor-trailing at the rear but revealing knees at the front. No doubt this would have worked well on our young Venetian lady, but on this woman—oh dear!

In Britain, at least, there seems to be little risk of formal dress disappearing altogether. Perhaps because of the continuity in our institutions, or perhaps because of a strong sense of nostalgia for a more glamorous past, we seem to derive considerable pleasure from kitting ourselves out in finery and making a splash (in more than one sense) at a special event. I think that this may be one explanation for the recent growth of summer opera festivals in and around grand country houses which I described in Chapter Two. Going to the opera has become a good excuse for dressing up, perhaps as much as dressing up has been a good excuse for going to the opera.

Although they may not share our obsession with formal dress, the approach of Americans is not dissimilar. I culled the following from a "How To Do Things" website.

"How to dress for an opera depends on the city tı in. For residents who live in the more casual pl. as Los Angeles, they will not be as adorned as tl attend an opera in New York. But, wherever you attend an opera, it's a big night out, and your dress reflect the magnitude of the event.

A night out at the opera is one of the best opportunities to wear the most elegant dress in your closet and be decked to the nines. One of the first rules is to wear an outfit that reflects your level of flamboyance. If you are an understated person, then a basic black dress splashed with a little jewellery for colour will do. For the woman who wants to step out in style, the opera is a place where this is expected. Try a full length gown, your best jewellery and a matching wrap."

Very sensible advice, not the least with its reference to the city lived in. When in 2003 I attended the first night of the season at the San Francisco Opera, I certainly felt the sense of occasion and the outfits on display accorded more with what the writer expects of New York than Los Angeles. The work given, Virgil Thomson's *The Mother Of Us All,* was less appropriate. The subject matter, the fight for female suffrage in the USA, might have been sufficiently American, but both the text by Gertrude Stein and Thomson's music were too elliptical for an audience whose presence was not wholly attributable to an interest in twentieth-century opera.

Incidentally, it would be wrong to assume that the larger or the more affluent the city, the dressier the audience. In my experience, in France and Germany, what is worn at small provincial opera houses, such as those in, for example, Metz or Pforzheim, tends to be more conservative, and therefore also more elegant, than that encountered in metropolitan Paris and Berlin. This is perhaps because the developments towards informality have been slower in the provinces; or because attending the opera there is more of a social convention and that encourages greater conformity.

question is often raised whether the social elitism traditionally associated with opera-going is inconsistent with the appreciation of opera as an art form. The answer to this is not straightforward. On the one hand, those able to afford only the cheaper seats upstairs tend, in my experience, to be more knowledgeable and perhaps also more involved in, and enthusiastic for, great performances. On the other hand, I have not been much bothered by the behaviour of those occupying the more expensive parts of the house. True, one can often spot corporate sponsors and their guests. The relevant row in the stalls or dress circle tends to be empty until the last moment, and when the occupants arrive, they are often noisy and seem already to be well lubricated. But once the lights are dimmed, they usually become like other members of the audience.

Admittedly, on one occasion, at a performance of *I Capuleti ed I Montecchi* by Bellini given by the Pimlico Opera at Salford's Lowry Theatre, I did have a problem with what I assume was a group of sponsors immediately in front of me. Throughout the first half, a couple were forever moving their heads together to whisper to each other. Because they were directly in my line of vision, it was impossible to ignore them and the fact that each little interchange was accompanied by a smile or smirk led me to believe that they were not taking entirely seriously Bellini's version of the Romeo and Juliet tragedy. When it got too much for me, I tapped one of them on the shoulder and asked if they would be kind enough to reserve their commentary for the interval. That seemed to do the trick but, in any event, they did not return for the second half.

I confess that I am not very tolerant of talking, persistent coughing, the unwrapping of sweet papers and other noises from fellow members of the audience. If they are behind me, I will typically turn round and glower at them. This ploy has often been effective, but not when, during a performance of Handel's *Orlando* at Covent Garden, it failed to deter the conversation of a French couple sitting near to me. The last straw was the ringing of their mobile telephone; yet even then they seem unperturbed by my exclamation "*Mais quand même!* ..."

Those in glass houses should not throw stones. I can also recall being myself reprimanded by an elderly woman in the row behind me for not keeping still. Helen and I were on our honeymoon and at the Operetta Festival in Bad Ischl, Austria. It has to be said that the Kongress und TheaterHaus where the performances take place is not ideal for the purpose, since the auditorium is simply a large rectangular room with no sloping floor. Because I was behind someone quite tall, and he kept moving his head, I had to move mine in the opposite direction in order to see the stage where *Der Vogelhändler* by Carl Zeller was being performed. I can understand how this combination of movements must have been irritating for the good lady behind me, but what else could I do?

If I were to make a generalisation concerning audience engagement in opera performances during my lifetime it would apply equally to the elite and the non-elite, to the affluent and the not-so-affluent: audiences tend now to be more attentive and more involved than they used to be. Two developments, in particular, are responsible for this. First, performances of opera have changed from being primarily a musical experience, hearing people sing, to a musical-theatrical experience. Greater demands have been made on the acting skills of singers and, through innovation in productions styles, this has enhanced the dramatic content of opera and made it more relevant to a contemporary public. Secondly, there has been the introduction of surtitles, the importance of which cannot be exaggerated.

Until the 1980s, performances in the international opera houses were mainly given in the original language of the work, while in other theatres they were often given in translation in the native language of the audience. Neither approach was entirely satisfactory. It can be assumed that only a (small) minority of the audience would be sufficiently familiar with a foreign language to be able to follow the text, word for word. True, diligent opera-goers would prepare for a performance by reading a synopsis of the plot, and sometimes even the libretto, in advance, but typically this meant only that they had a general sense of what was happening on stage. If, as is the case with many operas, it is important to understand exactly what is being sung—because the drama emerges as much through the text as through the music—then only a few could engage with the performance at this level. One consequence was that many producers and singers felt that they had to make a greater effort with bodily gestures to compensate for the difficulties of communicating to the audience through language. This was particularly a problem for comic operas, such as those by Mozart, since it tended to push performances towards coarser, physical humour which might undermine the subtler aspects of the work.

Opera in translation would seem to be the answer, but it is not always a satisfactory alternative. In the first place, the sound of the original language may be so closely linked to the musical idiom that the translation jars or seems wrong. For example, in Italian operas numerous characters, to articulate their distress, exclaim "O cielo" against a climactic musical phrase. It is a major challenge to find an effective English equivalent for this: try singing "Oh! Heavens!" to the same musical phrase and you will see what I mean.

It is also true that the quality of translations often leaves much to be desired. In my early opera-going days, at Sadlers Wells and elsewhere, I recall listening to stilted old-fashioned English and shuddering with embarrassment. Things have improved since then and there are some fine, modern idiomatic translations now in use. In any event, many original libretti are not literary masterpieces. There is the story of the Englishman who recounted to his French friend that he had recently heard Gounod's *Faust* in English and the translation had been ridiculously bad. "Ah, *mon ami,* but you ought to hear it sung in French!" had been the friend's retort.

Even if allowances are made for a corny text, you might not be able to hear enough of it, when sung, to justify it being translated. This is, of course, also a problem when operas are sung in the original, and Richard Strauss is reputed to have said that even when an audience is familiar with the language it is likely that they will only catch about thirty per cent of the text. It is particularly frustrating when an effort has been made to aid comprehension by translating a piece and you still cannot understand it. Finally, there is the fact that singers on the international circuit will generally not be prepared to invest time in learning a role in translation if they are unlikely to be engaged to sing that version again.

These points should not, perhaps, be exaggerated. It is true that I have heard some wonderful performances of opera in translation, particularly in my younger days when many British singers were renowned for their clear articulation—it now astonishes me to recall how much of the text came across in the famous Sadlers Wells performances of Wagner in the 1970s, conducted by Reginald Goodall. And yet those performances were never completely satisfying because they were not, as the Germans would say, *echt*, that is, true to the original. It is like watching Brigitte Bardot in a French film in a version that has been dubbed; however sexy the English or American female voice may be, it does not sound right.

Normally foreign language films are shown with subtitles, and nowadays surtitles (or supertitles as they are sometimes called) have become a very attractive alternative to translated opera. They were first used in Toronto and subsequently in New York in 1983 and very quickly they spread around the opera world. But they come in different forms and in different locations. They are usually projected onto a screen above the stage so, if you are at the front of the stalls, you may have to crane your neck upwards to see them. Sometimes they are placed at either side of the stage. This is an advantage if, as in La Monnaie at Brussels, the translations are given in two languages because it avoids squeezing both into a single screen. That theatre has to adopt a strict policy of neutrality between French and Flemish and so, in the first half of a performance, you will get one of the languages on the right and the other on the left; for the second half, the settings will be reversed. My favourite system is that operating at the Vienna Staatsoper and the New York Met: there is a little screen on the rear of the seat in front of you, and, by means of a switch, you can choose whether or not to have the titles illuminated and, if so, in which language.

In the 1980s the use of surtitles was much debated, their opponents filling the corresponded columns of the *Opera* magazine with complaints that they were a distraction and that they interfered with communication between singers and audience. Admittedly over-prominent titles can dominate the sightline of the stage and what is happening there. To counter this, the titles are sometimes dimmed. But this can be self-defeating, because if the titles are hard to read, your attention is diverted away from the stage for even longer periods. So also if there is too much to absorb; this can occur if the titles provide too literal a translation of the libretto. Ideally a quick glance should be sufficient to get the sense of the words being sung. Then there is the question of the timing of the surtitles. It is often difficult to get them to coincide exactly with the singing of the relevant phrase and hence the translation may appear before the words are sung. It is particularly irritating in comic opera if a funny line prematurely provokes laughter from the audience.

Nevertheless I think that these disadvantages are small relative to the huge benefits of enhanced comprehension, and opposition to surtitles seems almost to have disappeared. Audiences have come to depend on them. When, in June 2000, I attended a performance of Mussorgsky's *Khovanschina* at Covent Garden, given by the Kirov Opera (as it then was), the surtitle screen suddenly went blank towards the end of the First Act. The system was not restored and no explanation was given. I was furious and during the second interval sought out the House Manager to complain. By way of compensation I was offered a discount on another performance at Covent Garden. At the beginning of the Third Act, an apology was made from the front of the stage, though without mention of a discount—sometimes it pays to complain personally.

Technological advances have improved the effectiveness and reliability of surtitle systems. Presumably their cost has also been reduced because now even small touring companies operating on a shoestring budget seem to be able to afford a simple version. In the Autumn of 2009 the young Heritage Opera group toured the North of England with *Halka*, a work by the Polish composer Stanislaw Moniuszko. Though well known in its own country, *Halka* is a rarity here, and it was enterprising not only to offer it in venues like the Trinity Church at

Skipton, but also to have it sung in the original language. The presence of a couple of young Polish singers helped, but so did the projection of surtitles onto a small screen, a system which worked immaculately.

One aspect of surtitles remains controversial: should they be used for operas when the performance is given in the audience's own language? The English National Opera have struggled with this question, finally in 2005 acceding to public demand and making them available. Many opera houses elsewhere have reached the same decision and in Germany this has proved to be a blessing for the appreciation of works by Strauss and Wagner. Bayreuth has resisted the trend, doubtless expecting those who make the pilgrimage to the shrine to be sufficiently familiar with what is performed there. But this is a special case. The objection that surtitling encourages singers to be too complacent in their articulation may be right, but it is outweighed by the better understanding of the text.

This is particularly important for contemporary opera which often has a complex or sophisticated libretto. Over the years, when attempting to grapple with modern works, I have frequently been frustrated by the inability to hear the words above the music. In 1968, at the Edinburgh Festival, I saw *Punch and Judy* by Harrison Birtwistle in its original production by the English Opera Group. The two elderly Morningside ladies sitting next to me in the King's Theatre were completely bewildered by this violent piece and I suspect that, when buying tickets, they thought they were going to see a puppet Punch and Judy show, of the kind which one used to encounter on seaside piers. But although I had known what I was in for, I fared no better, simply because I could not sufficiently follow the text. And more recently the same problem has affected my appreciation of such apparently impressive works as *Powder Her Face,* the piece by Thomas Adès about the promiscuous Duchess of Argyll. In short, surtitling has been a marvellous means of ensuring greater audience appreciation of opera.

When, in 1977, I was asked by the German magazine *Orpheus* to review a Welsh National Opera performance of Verdi's *I Masnadieri* in Cardiff,

I drew the analogy between crossing the River Severn and crossing the Alps from Germany to Italy. My point was that Welsh opera audiences were as different from English opera audiences as Italian audiences were from German audiences. The Welsh share with the Italians the love of the sound of the singing voice. Listen to the speaking voice of great Welsh singers, such as Geraint Evans and Bryn Terfel, and you notice how the intonation and the sing-song quality make the language musical, a quality which transposes itself easily into, say, an Italian aria. So, overhearing the people around me in the Cardiff New Theatre (the WNO's base before the Wales Millennium Centre was built), I seemed already to be half way to Verdi's idiom. Add to that their emotional involvement in music, signalled first by their heartfelt rendering of the Welsh national anthem before the performance began, and then by their obvious relishing of the "in your face" singing of the soloists, and it is difficult to resist sharing their enjoyment.

Similarly, when, for one reason or another, an audience has a special interest in the performers and wills them to do well, involvement and enthusiasm can be infectious. This may arise when a performance has poignancy because of circumstances such as the reopening of a theatre after wartime, or after reconstruction following a fire. Maybe audience and performers alike have overcome bad weather conditions to get to the theatre. In November 2005 there was an unusually early fall of snow in north-west Germany and, for a performance of Weber's *Der Freischütz,* the theatre at Krefeld was only half full. I recall being mightily impressed by what I saw and heard. But it is unclear to what extent this was due to the quality of the production and musical interpretation. My judgement might have been induced by gratitude, shared by the small audience, that the show had gone on under difficult circumstances.

Then a performance may have sentimental value because the artists are particular favourites of the audience. This was clearly the case when in 1979 I saw at the Coliseum Handel's *Julius Caesar* with Janet Baker and Valerie Masterson and conducted by Charles Mackerras. So also when in 2007 Pierre Boulez, aged 82, was in Aix-en-Provence, reunited with his old sparring partner Patrice Chéreau in their production of Janáček's *From the House of the Dead*. In these cases you could almost feel goodwill emanating from the seats around you.

A not dissimilar atmosphere often attaches to opera performances given by students or non-professionals. Of course, there may be many friends and family present but, quite apart from this, benevolence may result from the audience recognising that opera is a demanding challenge for the group in question. Such may occur when there is a risk that, by being ambitious, they may have bitten off more than they can chew. In the 1970s I went several times to the annual opera production at the University of Reading, and the warmth of the reception seemed quite justified for the boldness in putting on, with limited resources, Verdi's *La Battaglia di Legnano*, Glinka's *Ruslan and Ludmilla*, Schubert's *Alfonso und Estrella* and César Franck's *Hulda*.

More recently I have regularly attended performances given by students at the Royal Northern College of Music at Manchester. Here audience goodwill would appear to have another explanation. There is widespread acknowledgement that the College provides one of the best training centres in Britain for singers, and the quality of the performances is typically so high that there is a much local pride in, and identification with, the achievements of the young participants. Add to this that, with scouts around on the lookout for promising talent, the students are eager to impress and energetically throw themselves into the performance, and you can understand why there is invariably an audience buzz at the RNCM.

The opera-going public obviously varies from one location to another. Those in Paris can be quite eccentric. As I was leaving the Palais Garnier in 1966 after a performance of *Un Ballo in Maschera*, an elderly lady in a long gown exclaimed loudly to her companion, so that all around could hear, *"Ma chère, c'était sublime"*. And this was in the bad old days at the Paris Opéra, when the offerings were old-fashioned and mediocre. Sometimes it is at the other extreme. After Rolf Liebermann had been imported from Hamburg to transform things, I was back in Paris in the summer of 1973 for *Il Trovatore*, conducted by our own, and fondly remembered, Edward Downes. As he arrived in the pit after the interval, and asked the orchestra to stand to share in the applause, someone in the audience shouted out, "*l'orchestre à la poubelle*", suggesting that the orchestra should be removed to the dustbin, a judgement which I considered to be most unfair.

In Germany, audiences in the bigger houses can be demonstrative, whether, in a positive sense, favouring a performance, or negatively, disapproving of it. In the smaller houses, they tend to be restrained. This can be disappointing. In March 1996 I travelled from Hamburg to Rostock to see *Don Carlos*, one of my favourite operas. Rostock is a Hanseatic port on the north-east coast. It was somewhat run-down, and when I was there was best known for football, having at that time the only East German team in the Bundesliga. Certainly its cultural activities seemed to be at a low ebb, because the theatre was three-quarters empty. And those that did attend failed to appreciate what a good performance was taking place, in particular because the director Manfred Straube and designer Franziska Harbort provided a visually striking production that was able to contrast the private and public spheres of the work.

When it was announced in 2006 that the company which had mounted the excellent *Freischütz* in Krefeld were to give, in Mönchengladbach, the world première of an opera entitled *Das Frauenorchester von Auschwitz* (The Women's Orchestra of Auschwitz), I was intrigued. I had read about the group of female musicians who had been saved from slaughter by playing for their Nazi masters—they included Anita Lasker who was later to emigrate to Britain, marry the pianist Peter Wallfisch and produce a remarkable musical family. How could an opera on such a topic be composed and performed? And how would it feel to be a member of an audience in Germany for such a work? To get answers to these questions, I decided to go and see it.

The music, by a young German composer Stefan Heucke, was powerful, as was the production, but unsurprisingly the work failed to measure up to the scale of the horrors which had been perpetrated in the death camps. What then of the audience? The theatre was not full but there were still many people there. They were reserved and applauded politely at the end, but I could get no sense of how they were feeling inside, and emerged from the evening with little addition to my understanding of the Germans and the whys and wherefores of the Holocaust. Still, it was very striking, even reassuring, that a small opera company in Germany was willing to put on a work of this kind.

At Maastricht in 2004 I attended the première of a production of Wagner's *Fliegende Holländer* given by the Opera Zuid company. The performance was of average quality and I noticed that the foreign singers in the cast (they included the Britons Mark Beesley and Adrian Thompson) appeared somewhat surprised when, at the end, the Dutch audience rose to applaud them. Was the performance really such, they must have asked themselves, as to deserve a standing ovation? No doubt, afterwards, it would have been explained to them that at the end of almost all performances the Dutch stand up to clap. I have never accustomed myself to this habit and unless really impressed by what I have seen and heard, I rather grumpily stay seated. I also dislike it when, in Belgium and sometimes elsewhere, ordinary applause develops into rhythmic, synchronised clapping. Perhaps this is because to me it is reminiscent of the regimented mass displays organised in totalitarian regimes. In any event, it implies a lack of individual judgement.

I should not wish, however, to give the impression that I am restrained in my appreciation at the opera. Far from it; I am wont to cheer performers who have excelled. Though perhaps I am not entirely consistent in my behaviour. I am more likely to bellow my *bravo* in a small or provincial theatre where the expectations are not so high, and where cheering is less familiar than in international houses where it is commonplace and where some singers might be acclaimed simply because they are famous and the audience have paid a lot to hear them. So also, if I particularly like the orchestra and the interpretation of the music, I tend to cheer conductors whose qualities are often appreciated less than those of singers.

Of course some audiences tend to be more discriminating than others. In my experience those at Covent Garden, Vienna and Munich make reliable judgements, although this may simply mean that I tend to agree with them. The same probably applies to La Scala, but not necessarily elsewhere in Italy. Incidentally, if you are in that country, you should note the importance of grammar. The exact word used for the acclamation will depend on who is being cheered: if it is *bravo,* it will be for one male performer; *brava* for one female performer; *brave* for two or more females; and *bravi* for two or more males (or a mix of males and females).

In some theatres, you may get the feeling that the cheers are not entirely spontaneous. Have they been orchestrated in some way? Is there a *claque* in the house? The days when singers were known to pay people for vigorous applause are supposed to be over (for a wonderful, amusing account of how the *claque* operated at the Vienna Staatsoper in the 1920s, you should read Joseph Wechsberg's autobiography *Looking for a Bluebird*). But sometimes applause, when it is inappropriately enthusiastic, makes one wonder.

A *claque* can be effective because of a well-known feature of audience behaviour: many people will follow the lead taken by some individuals and therefore it is not difficult to influence the reaction of audiences to particular performers. But it is also a matter of good timing. You must shout out just before most people decide how much they will applaud. I put this to the test when I was at a performance of Handel's *Alcina* in Düsseldorf in 2002. The soprano Alexandra von der Weth, who had mightily impressed me two years earlier when she sang Fiordiligi at Glyndebourne, gave a marvellous interpretation of the title role. It was not a large audience—Handel's operas were at that time not very popular in Germany—and I suspected that the worthy citizens of Düsseldorf were insufficiently aware of their good fortune in having such an outstanding singer as a member of their ensemble. So, just as she appeared for her bow at the end, and before the applause had started, I shouted my *bravo.* I was very pleased when she received a very warm reception from the rest of the small audience.

Audience appreciation at the end of the performance is different from when it occurs during a performance, say at the end of an aria. In the old days interventions of this kind were usual in all opera houses and are still common in many today. Inducing such behaviour was a principal function of the *claque*, since a salvo of applause immediately after an aria could be expected to get the audience to think that they were experiencing a great performance; it would also provide encouragement for the singers themselves. But here, even more than at the end of the performance, timing was crucial. A shout of *bravo* emitted too early might spoil the impact of the music; and if it were held back too long, it would give the impression of not being spontaneous. Members of the *claque* had, therefore, to know the score well. Wechsberg relates how, for *claquers*, *Carmen* was a "difficult" opera because there would be frequent pauses when they had to elicit applause; but Wagner operas were "easy" because the music is continuous and there was nothing to do until the end of each Act.

I have mixed feelings about applauding individual numbers. If it occurs during baroque and early nineteenth-century opera, the musical continuity is not broken and some of the arias are, and were intended to be, showpieces for the singers. On the other hand, opera productions have increasingly moved away from the purely musical to integrated drama and music, and interruptions can break the spell of theatrical illusion. It can also encourage singers to behave indulgently, "milking" the climax to an aria in order to gain more applause. Even worse, audiences may begin to applaud at the end of the vocal part but before the orchestra has finished its accompaniment. This does not happen often but, when it does, it is intolerable, particularly with a composer like Handel where the orchestral line is integral to the resolution of the musical phrasing. I experienced it at the London Coliseum during a performance in 1992 of Nicholas Hytner's famous and delectable production of *Xerxes*. I was so angry that I asked the person sitting next to me in the stalls if he would hold back his applause until the orchestra finished. He did, but since hundreds of others in the audience continued with the awful practice, my little protest was to no avail.

How do, and should, opera audiences show displeasure at what they have heard and seen? There has been a long tradition of booing and whistling in opera houses, particularly in France and Italy. Historically, much of it was the result of factions among the opera-going public. For example, when Rossini ventured to write a work based on the Beaumarchais play *The Barber of Seville*, this offended the supporters of Giovanni Paisello, a rival composer, who had already produced a very successful version of the same work. They ensured that the première of Rossini's opera at Rome in 1816 was a failure by hissing and jeering throughout. Then there might be competing *claques* promoting and opposing rival singers. This was the case already in Handel's time in London, notably involving the soprano Francesca Cuzzoni and the mezzo Faustina Bordoni. A performance of an opera by Bononcini came to a halt when a fight on stage broke out between the two factions. Even in more recent times, in the 1950s, the fans of Maria Callas at La Scala made it difficult for other sopranos singing roles for which she had become famous.

The wrath of audiences could also be provoked if a composer failed to observe dearly held conventions. When Wagner rewrote *Tannhäuser* for Paris in 1861, he inserted a ballet in the First Act. Now members of the wealthy, highly influential, Jockey Club, who were particularly attached to the ballet, normally arrived at opera only for the beginning of the Second Act, to give themselves time to finish their dinner. So when a group of them arrived at *Tannhäuser* only to find that they had missed the ballet, they expressed their discontent with whistles and catcalls. premièrePolitics and ideology can also be involved. In 1932 the Nazis were a powerful force in Berlin but could not yet dictate what was to be performed in the theatres, so the next best strategy was to disrupt what they disapproved of. By means of an anti-semitic demonstration, they were able to ruin, for example, the premiere of Franz Schreker's opera *Der Schmied von Gent*.

In more recent times, audiences have rarely displayed open hostility to composers and their works. That may seem surprising given the array of strange, and often incomprehensible, pieces which have been presented in opera houses. Perhaps this is because those attending performances of anti-operas and the like are typically not numerous, and presumably have a pretty good idea, before they enter the theatre, of what they are in for.

Open disapproval of singers does sometimes occur in Italy where the public, in such places as Parma, are known to be severe critics of vocal technique. In December 2006 the famous tenor Roberto Alagna was booed at Milan's La Scala during a performance of Aida and he stormed off the stage, refusing to continue. He later threatened to sue the opera house for failing to protect him against damage, claiming that his blood sugar level had dropped dangerously low as a result of his distress.

Although during my years of opera-going I have experienced some pretty awful vocal performances, I do not recall a singer being booed in this way, and I am pleased to have avoided it. It is true that much money is spent on tickets in international house to hear great voices and it is irritating when what actually materialises is far below one's expectations. But most singers have occasional "off-days" and they should not be punished when this occurs. Booing is even crueller when a famous singer has had to be replaced, and the substitute is of a disappointingly lower standard. Both practices can seriously affect a singer's career because the human voice is a vulnerable instrument and can respond badly to stress or a loss of confidence.

Some booing should not be taken seriously. In Britain there is a tradition of doing this when the villain in a piece comes on for his bow. The practice is derived from pantomime and sometimes occurs in opera. Although foreign singers may have been taken aback when first encountering it, they soon learn that it is done as part of the theatrical entertainment and has nothing to do with the quality of performance.

Nevertheless I must now make a confession. Once, at an opera performance, Catherine and I were so angry with a singer that when he appeared at the end for his bow we booed, though not very loudly and he may not have heard. He played Don Alfonso in *Cosi Fan Tutte* when Scottish Opera gave this piece at Newcastle in 1982. It was a revival of the famous production, directed by Anthony Besch and designed by John Stoddart, which had originally been created for Elizabeth Harwood and Janet Baker and it was a model of refined and elegant comic opera. The interpretation of the other members of the cast, which included Margaret Marshall and Ann Murray, matched perfectly this approach. In contrast, the vulgarity and coarseness of the Don Alfonso stuck out like a sore thumb. But please note that we were highly critical of his physical acting, not his singing, and I doubt whether our outburst could have affected his career in the way described above.

In modern times, it has been undoubtedly opera production which has generated most audience hostility. Productions tend to be controversial because, as we shall see in Chapter Nine, directors and designers have increasingly taken liberties in interpreting works so that what is performed may radically depart from what the composer and librettist intended. Although some opera-goers may have no problem with this, others may find the new interpretation illegitimate, inappropriate or simply inconsistent with the music. So also the objection might be that, interesting or not, the staging is exaggerated, vulgar or ugly. While these developments have occurred throughout the opera world, they are most frequently encountered in Germany where, in the larger houses, almost every new production is greeted by a mixture of boos from its opponents, and cheers from its supporters; though obviously the relative strength of each will vary from case to case.

I do not frequently attend first nights and so have rarely faced the dilemma of whether or not to participate in demonstrations of this kind. But when I was in Hanover, in 2010, at the premiere of a new production of Mozart's *Die Entführung aus dem Serail,* which I found both insightful and moving, I joined in the cheers, hoping that that would make them louder than the boos. Conversely, the 1999 production of *Elektra* by Richard Strauss at Aachen was so ugly, with human worms crawling around the stage, that I made some sort of unpleasant noise when the director Claus Schmitz appeared at the end.

If you have strong opinions on a production and wish to vent your feelings, but it is not the first night and so the production team of director and designer do not appear, what should you do? If you do not wish the singers and conductor to be implicated in your hostility, you have only one realistic possibility. You must boo, whistle or whatever when the music has stopped and the curtain has come down, but before the performers appear on the stage for their bow. At the Bavarian State Opera in Munich, in October 2010, the audience demonstrated this approach to perfection. The opera was a rarity, *Media in Corinto*, by Giovanni Simone Mayr, a contemporary of Beethoven. It was difficult to judge the quality of the music because the awfulness of the production, by Hans Neuenfels, was too distracting. The director was concerned more to provoke his audience than to convey insights on the work. Yes, ancient Greece was a cruel world, but we could understand that without the series of gory deaths and savage rapes, piled on to such a degree that the stomach turned. So when the curtain came down on the First Act, there were howls of disgust and, although I did not join in, I sympathised with them.

Another way of expressing your opinion is, after the performance, to upload a blog on an appropriate website, or send a letter or email to the company's artistic director. In my experience, if you do the latter you are unlikely to receive a satisfactory reply. In 2004 I had the misfortune to see, at the Deutsche Oper Berlin, another disastrous production by Herr Neuenfels, this time of Verdi's *Il Trovatore*. I shall have more to say about this in Chapter Nine. Suffice it here to note that I was so outraged by what I saw that I subsequently wrote a letter to Kirsten Harms, the *Intendantin* of the theatre, listing my objections to the staging. Frau Harms courteously replied, but it was a bland response, not addressing any of the points I had made. She simply observed that the company performed with a variety of production styles, and hoped that I would return to see something which would please me more.

More often, I have received no answer to letters of complaint. This can be somewhat frustrating, but in 1985 I was even more irritated by a response signed by John Cox, then Artistic Director of Scottish Opera. It related to Graham Vick's production of *Don Giovanni* which I had seen in Newcastle. This was a staging given in a contemporary setting which I found riveting and very true to the spirit of the original. But it had not been widely liked, and when I learned that many letters of complaint had been sent, I wrote to say how much I had appreciated the production. In his response, Mr Cox expressed his regret that some people had been offended by Graham Vick's approach and wished to reassure me that the policy of the company was to respect the composer's intentions. Obviously no one at Scottish Opera had read my letter. I was furious.

The director David Pountney, when he was head of productions at the English National Opera, once said that he welcomed booing because it showed that that the audience were engaged, rather than passive, and that a difference of opinion on how works should be interpreted was healthy. I do not believe that in practice directors and designers actually enjoy being confronted by demonstrations of this kind on first nights but, considered from a more abstract perspective, I think that he is right. Whether inspired by love or hate, audience involvement is important to opera.

CHAPTER SEVEN

COMPOSERS

Suppose you were taking your niece or granddaughter to her first opera, which composer would you choose for the initiation? Limiting your choice to some of the major opera composers, whom would you select of the following, listed more or less in chronological order: Handel, Mozart, Wagner, Verdi, Puccini or Janáček?

I would take a safe bet that you would not go for Handel (almost nothing but solo arias), Wagner (too long-winded) or Janáček (too modern with difficult harmonies). Any of the other three are possible, but in Mozart the drama is subject to the stop-start of recitative and arias or ensembles, while Verdi's plots are often corny and unconvincing. So I suspect that many would opt for Puccini, say, *La Bohème, Madam Butterfly,* or *Tosca.*

As I indicated in Chapter One, my first experience of opera in the theatre was Britten, but I would have done much better with Puccini. Why so? Most obviously because of the accessibility of his musical idiom: he had such a gift for writing great lyrical melodies, particularly for the soprano and tenor voices as they soar above the sound of the orchestra. There is also the emotional intensity which he is able to generate for familiar situations of love and betrayal. The plot is tightly structured; it is made up of strong meaty stuff, and easily grasped: you do not have to search for a "meaning". Singing is part of the drama and the music is continuous, not broken up into separate numbers, and so you are less aware of the artifice of composition. It is *verismo* opera, seeking to portray real people in realistic settings. And perhaps this helps those coming to opera for the first time to enter fully into the experience of musical drama.

One of the problems which besets Puccini performances is, paradoxically, the result of their being so successful. Because the operas are so popular, company managers are wont to wheel them out when they need to increase box office receipts. Also, if the public are happy with an existing production, why waste money in creating a new one? After all, one traditional realistic production is more or less like any other. When I first saw *La Bohème* at Covent Garden in 1965, the decor was the same as that used when Nellie Melba sang Mimi there before and after the First World War. And you will recall, from Chapter Three, that the Hamburg State Opera's production of *Madam Butterfly* created in 1966 was still being performed in 2010. Since *verismo* opera must be convincing at the level of realism, the perpetuation of stale old productions undermines the effectiveness of the genre.

In the last twenty years or so, new life has been injected into the performances of some Puccini operas through the astute updating of productions. If audiences are able to identify more easily with the updated period than that of the original, this can enhance the effectiveness of *verismo* opera. But, back in the 1970s, as my experience of opera grew, so the attractions of *verismo* begin to wane. This may be because Puccini's method of churning up the emotions, with the aid of a big tune, becomes a little predictable and formulaic. Perhaps even more importantly I started to question the merits of the realistic approach to musical theatre. If trueness to life is the test, then gritty films like *Saturday Night and Sunday Morning* or *A Streetcar Named Desire* might pass with flying colours, but opera cannot work at this level, most obviously because people do not normally go around communicating their thoughts and emotions through singing. And if opera cannot imitate real life, should we not be looking for something more in it?

For me, a key moment in appreciating this came during a performance of *La Bohème* at the London Coliseum in 1977. I was, at the time, the British correspondent of the Berlin opera magazine *Orpheus* and had been asked to review the new ENO production by the French director Jean-Claude Auvray. Now, for the most part, there was nothing unusual in Auvray's approach. The sets and costumes were faithful to mid-nineteenth-century Paris; indeed, you can hardly have had a more realistic Café Momus than that presented on the stage. But at moments, when the inner thoughts of Rodolfo, Mimi or Marcello were being revealed to the audience, the lighting changed: while the characters in question were strongly illuminated, things around them became dark and still.

I found this theatrically very effective, and in my review I suggested that the non-realistic effect helped in drawing together important unifying themes in the drama—fidelity and remorse, for example— which otherwise might get submerged under the external events which dominate the piece. My review was never published. I was disputing with the editors of *Orpheus* about other matters and they told me that, in any event, my observations about the production reflected my inexperience. Everyone knows, they said, that *La Bohème* is a model of dramatic construction and does not need special effects to make it work—and I was fired. Whatever the rights and wrongs of this incident—I recall that Harold Rosenthal, the renowned editor of the British magazine *Opera*, reviewing the same production found the lighting effects irritating and inappropriate—it did show how Puccini's operas do not easily lend themselves to a non-realistic approach. It also was a good indication of my growing conviction that production styles which eschewed realism might be more satisfying.

The composer whom I idolised in my earlier opera-going years was Wagner. I started my Wagnerian adventure with *Die Meistersinger*— appropriately because, being set in a relatively recent and recognisable historical period of the sixteenth century, it was about real people; and productions could, and still can, succeed with a realist approach. I recall, at the age of eighteen, being bowled over by the finale to the work, as (it seemed) all of Nuremberg gathered on the Covent Garden stage to hail and honour Great Art. But I was moved also by the lyricism and humanity of the piece, particularly in the first half of the Second Act when the warmth of the summer night pervades the music and seems to imbue the characters with gentleness and what the Germans call *Gemütlichkeit* (not easily translated, but a combination of cosiness, cheerfulness and social belonging).

Thereafter I became responsive to the brilliance of Wagner's orchestral writing. Reading Bernard Levin's highly entertaining book, *Conducted Tour*, I found that he went though the same phase. When, as a young man, he heard "the opening bars of the Prelude to *Tristan*, or the merest growl from Fafner as a snatch of *Siegfried* passes by, or the shimmering wonder of the Good Friday Spell from *Parsifal*, the passion flares up, and in a few seconds [he was] once again drunk beyond breathalysers". More than this, there was the scale of Wagner's enterprise, his goal of reaching out to a *Weltanschauung* ("world view"), by means of *Gesamtkunstwerk* (a synthesis of art forms—music, drama, design). Yes, I know, this is all very German, but Wagner was very German.

When I moved onto the *Ring*, a new perspective unfolded. I became captivated by the Wagnerian system of composition, the *leitmotifs*. By linking musical themes to characters, events, ideas and emotions, the composer was able to provide an orchestral commentary on the drama. This could become quite nuanced as variations in the motif might, for example, suggest a development or tension in a character's predicament. Or, while the individual might be singing one thing, the orchestra, by means of a relevant motif, may tell us that she is thinking of something else. There is also an open-endedness to the "meaning" of the motifs. The downward phrase in the woodwinds which often recurs during Wotan's monologues is often referred to as the "Spear-motif", but other commentators call it the "Treaty-motif", indicating the obligations which obstruct the God's will; and in a broader sense it can refer to limits on the ability of people to determine their own destiny.

In preparation for attending a performance at Covent Garden in 1965, my pal Robin and I spent hours listening to Decca's recently issued recording of *Siegfried*, conducted by Solti. I followed what was happening in the Breitkopf vocal score of the work which helpfully inserted little numbers in the music to indicate where and when a motif was to be heard. Robin would have a libretto at hand and I would shout out the name of the motif as it was played. If the reason for that particular motif was not obvious, we might, when the disc had come to an end, discuss its significance: "Hey, Robin, when Siegfried tells Wotan that he's off to find Brünnhilde, did you hear the Rhinemaidens' motif? Why do you think that was?"

A few years later, I devised my "Wagner Conversion Sessions". I invited round friends who had had no previous experience of the composer. A bust of Wagner was placed in the corner of the room and in front of it a lighted candle. I played for my guests carefully selected extracts from *Die Walküre*, the most accessible and "human" of the Ring dramas. These included much of the First Act, culminating in the love scene between Siegmund and Sieglinde, the *Todesverkünden* scene where Brünnhilde announces to Siegmund his forthcoming death in battle; and, of course, at the end, the Fire Music and Wotan's very beautiful Farewell to Brünnhilde. I would start by identifying for my invitees the motifs as they were played, but as the evening progressed would allow them to wallow in the music. I cannot say how many people I actually converted to Wagner and on one occasion I had to pretend that I had not noticed that a friend had fallen asleep during the *Todesverkünden* scene; but I, at least, thoroughly enjoyed the sessions.

If I have not yet convinced you of my Wagnermania during these years, two further episodes should do the trick. In 1972, when I purchased my first house, I gave it the name Nibelheim, the place in the depths of the earth where the dwarf Alberich works to create forces which would give him power over the world. This was admittedly a bit daft, but I could hardly call it Walhalla, the legendary home of the Gods. Then in 1977, when I was invited by the Director of a Research Institute in Munich to give a lecture on "Social Security in Britain since the Second World War", I decided to interpret my subject matter by reference to the *Ring*. So William Beveridge, the architect of the Welfare State, became Wotan, and the task of setting the system to rights in the 1970s was entrusted to Brünnhilde, in the person of Barbara Castle, who at that time was Secretary of State for Health and Social Security and was planning a major reform of pensions. I even found an equivalent for the Waldvogel, the little bird which in *Siegfried* leads the hero to find Brünnhilde, but I cannot now remember which worthy proponent of welfare reform was deemed to assume this role.

As had happened to Bernard Levin, my euphoria with Wagner was not to last. Like him, I became a little resistant, partly through uneasiness about the composer's ideology which, apart from his music, led him to be so revered by the Nazis. In 1969, I should have taken more notice of the remarks of my flatmate, Wolfgang. As a German intellectual, brought up in the post-war period, he was typically left-wing and alienated by much traditional culture. He introduced me to jazz, but had never been to a Wagner performance. I took him to *Meistersinger* at Covent Garden and his comment on the last scene, with its celebration of German Art and Life, and which I had so admired when I had first seen the work, was that it reminded him of the Nuremberg Rallies.

I ignored this and tried to overlook the composer's manifest anti-Semitism. I considered, and to some extent still consider, that the creative output of a genius like Wagner transcends his own personality and beliefs. But however I interpreted his mature works, I could not get away from the fact that they contained characters—Alberich, Mime, Beckmesser—that were obviously the result of racism and whose stage depiction displays an unpleasant degree of *schadenfreude*.

An even more important reason for the waning of my Wagnermania was the familiar phenomenon that, as you get older and your taste matures, you tend to prefer understatement to overstatement and to find more satisfying smaller-scale works that can make their impact without "in your face" effects. I have continued to see and to relish many Wagner performances, but other composers have reduced his hold on me. For example, Mozart …

There is no way of avoiding the admission that in my early opera-going days, I went to Mozart more out of respect and duty, than for love. To begin with, I was not wild about Mozart's music generally since I found it too predictable and it did not have the passion and scale of nineteenth-century romanticism, nor the power of the twentieth-century masterpieces. Then, though I much enjoyed *Die Zauberflöte*, which was exotic and fun, I did not get on too well with the Da Ponte operas, *Figaro*, *Don Giovanni* and *Cosi Fan Tutte*. The performances of these pieces that I attended in the 1960s at Covent Garden were starry affairs (Tito Gobbi, Geraint Evans, Mirella Freni, Teresa Berganza and so on), but the productions seemed to me to be too traditional, over-dressed and rather ponderous.

Another important reason for my coolness at the time was that my knowledge of the libretti was not sufficiently good to have been able to follow the dialogue in Italian, surtitles of course not being then available. The complexities of the plot of *The Marriage of Figaro*, for example, are considerable and even though I have now seen the opera eighteen times, I still have to concentrate carefully to understand at a certain point who is writing a letter to whom, and why. Admittedly, back in the 1960s, there were plenty of performances of the operas in English, at Sadlers Wells and elsewhere, but the translations were not brilliant and lacked the sparkle of the Italian original.

The breakthrough came in 1978, what was for me an *annus mirabilis* for Mozart operas. It was helped by the fact that my French girlfriend Catherine had come to live with me and she adored these works, knowing the major ones almost by heart. Then, good chance meant that I was able to see, in that year, several performances which revealed the depth of the Mozart–da Ponte exploration of human relationships. This happens as much through the musical idiom as through the text, the phrasing in the arias reflecting the inner emotions while the ensembles brilliantly set off one character's responses to a situation against those of the others.

Nowhere can one experience this more than in the second half of *Cosi Fan Tutte,* as what starts out as a silly game by two chaps to test the fidelity of their girls darkens as all four characters struggle with desire and jealousy. Although I had seen the piece several times before, Peter Hall's production at Glyndebourne was a revelation because he was careful to constrain the comedy and thus to make me realise that *Cosi* is, or can be played as, a serious piece. And he was helped by the delightful designs of John Bury, with their warm reds and browns, suggesting that love frolics are not all fun and joy. Now, you may argue, this is to misinterpret what Mozart intended, which was nothing other than a skit on female fickleness. My answer is that, whether or not this was the case, it does not matter. In the hands of a genius, works of art often turn out to be much more than their author had planned.

Two weeks previously I had been to the Cheltenham Festival for the Kent Opera production of another comic opera, *Die Entführung aus dem Serail.* The piece is set in a Turkish harem and is often played as a romp, the Western characters, in the midst of sensuous belly dancers, trying to outwit eunuchs and rotund soldiers in fez and tassel. But this was a production by Elijah Moshinsky whose *Lohengrin* and *Peter Grimes* at Covent Garden had both been mightily impressive for slimming down the works to their bare essentials, thereby enabling us to focus on the inner drama. His *Seraglio* was dark and severe, bringing to the foreground the tension between Western expectations of Islamic tyranny and the values of the Enlightenment. These values are in fact held by the Turk Pasha Selim, who, though he is thwarted in his love for the heroine Constanze, grants her freedom. The work may be a Singspiel, but the conductor, Roger Norrington, was able to demonstrate that beneath the surface of the light, pacy score, there is passion and nobility.

What these performances had made me realise was that Mozartian comic operas were not that simple. In terms of drama, they got to the heart of the human condition and, as regards music, there was something very satisfying in the way that the melodies and harmonies communicated emotions. To repudiate my erstwhile claim of predictability, the 1978 performance at Covent Garden of *Idomeneo* under Colin Davis came as a revelation. Listening to the surprising harmonies in the orchestra, and the brilliant instrumentation, demonstrated how wrong I had been.

The Davis *Idomeneo* also made me rethink my attitude to *opera seria*. This, the most typical style of opera in the baroque period, concentrates on solo, often *da capo,* arias, that is, written with an A-B-A structure, and reduces ensembles to the minimum. I had always found that the dominance of form and the lack of variety imposed a straitjacket on musical expression and the results were often boring. As I will relate, in time I would relish this artistic form especially when it was exploited with such brilliance by Handel; the Covent Garden performance was an important step in that direction.

Exploring Mozart's earlier output, you come across much *opera seria*, some of it better than others. When Catherine and I were in Wexford in 1989 to see *Mitridate* for the first time, we feared the worst. Mozart was only fourteen when he wrote this piece. When I thought what I had been up to (or perhaps down to) at that age, I could not believe that the experience would be worthwhile. Some months previously I had listened to part of a studio performance of the work broadcast by the BBC. Between the musical numbers, an announcer narrated the plot. This contained such absurdities that the audience began to titter and, as the performance progressed, it was very clear that the announcer was finding it very difficult to keep a straight face.

Our performance was on Sunday and the little theatre was only half full—presumably most of those who had come for the weekend had already left or felt that they would not be able to cope with nearly three-and-a-half hours of *opera seria*. Moreover, the previous evening we had sat through an awful production of *Der Templar und die Jüdin* (a version of Walter Scott's *Ivanhoe* by Heinrich Marschner, the German romantic composer); and with the presumably puerile *Mitridate* still to come, we were prepared to write off 1989 as a bad year for Wexford. In fact,

Mitridate proved to be a highlight of all of our Wexford experiences. The virtuosity of the vocal writing is breathtaking, requiring acrobatic accuracy, and we were rewarded by brilliant performances from the sopranos Cynthia Sieden and Laura Bybee, and the tenor Martin Thompson. If the melodrama involving sibling rivalry is somewhat rudimentary, Lucy Bailey, the director, nevertheless made the piece affecting rather than ridiculous, by a simple, powerful staging in which the physical movements of the singers matched the intensity of their vocal delivery.

Being almost a household name (Joe Green) Giuseppe Verdi is understandably a very popular opera composer—that cannot be said of Richard Bouquet, John Philip Branch, Arnold Fairhill, Claude Greenhill, Christopher Joy, Charles Weaver or even Richard Wheelwright (how many of these can you identify?). *Rigoletto* was the first opera I ever heard because my mother had been given as a present the famous recording with Maria Callas, Tito Gobbi and Giuseppe di Stefano, conducted by Tullio Serafin. I did not make much of it at the age of fifteen, and, indeed was, for a time, rather dismissive of Verdi's music which I found to be predominantly rum-ti-tum and, as such, hardly distinguishable from Arthur Sullivan's music for the Gilbert and Sullivan operas. Then I listened to *Don Carlos* on disc and at last I discovered something worthy of competing with Wagner, my idol of those years. (Incidentally, the relationship between the two composers was the theme of an excellent novel by Franz Werfel, a book which has been sadly neglected in the English-speaking world.)

What struck me first in *Don Carlos* was Verdi's ability to capture, in King Philip's great monologue in the first scene of Act Four, *Ella giammai mamo*, the introverted emotions of an individual who has to cope with problematic personal relationships as well as hostility from political opponents. But the whole of that scene is a miracle of musical-dramatic inventiveness from the extraordinary duologue for two basses, as the King is challenged by the Grand Inquisitor, through an exquisite quartet (*Ah, si maledetto, sospetto fatale*), to the final and justifiably famous aria for Eboli, *O don fatale*, perhaps the greatest piece written for a mezzo-soprano in nineteenth-century opera.

Over the years, I have seen *Don Carlos* many times and have often found it a most rewarding experience. This is, I think, mainly because opera companies treat the work as something special. It does not have the popular appeal of *Rigoletto, La Traviata* or *Aida*, and needs to be strongly cast, not only to meet the considerable demands of the work but also to pull in the public. I have heard some of the best singers of their generation in the piece including, at Covent Garden in 1966, Gwyneth Jones, Rita Gorr, Bruno Prevedi, Peter Glossop and Boris Christoff, and in 1977, Katia Ricciarelli, Grace Bumbry, Jose Carreras, Yuri Mazurok and Nicolai Ghiaurov; at San Francisco in 1992, Carol Vaness, Nina Terentieva, Richard Margison, Thomas Allen and Robert Lloyd; and at Vienna in 2003, Miriam Gauci, Violeta Urmana, Luis Lima, Carlo Alvarez and Samuel Ramey.

Singers of such quality are thin on the ground and this is, I believe, one important reason why performances of his other mature works (apart from the comic opera *Falstaff* which is more of an ensemble piece) have often been disappointing. Verdi requires voices capable of spinning long legato lines and also of having the "heft" to give the phrasing its emotional impact. Now a good production can compensate for some musical shortcomings but here again, in my experience, Verdi has not fared too well. Until he teamed up with Arrito Boito as his librettist, most of his operas were uneven, sometimes ramshackle, affairs containing glorious episodes but not always adding up to a coherent whole. The same can be said, of course, of many "straight" plays, including some of Shakespeare's, and a strong directorial hand is needed to turn them into powerful drama.

But a strong directorial hand has not often been there. Sadly, at a time when, under Peter Hall's inspired leadership, the Royal Shakespeare Company was establishing a new approach to epic theatre, almost none of this spilled over to the staging of Verdi opera, and performances were often little more than singers prepared to "stand and deliver" before heavy pseudo-realistic sets. For my first *Trovatore*, in 1965, Covent Garden had engaged Carlo Bergonzi, perhaps the finest Verdi tenor of the day, as Manrico. He sang divinely, but his ambling around the stage was, to put it mildly, unconvincing as drama. This might not have been a surprise to those who three years earlier had seen him at the same theatre in *La Forza del Destino*. With unusual enterprise, the management had invited Sam Wanamaker to direct; and he responded with a pared-down Brechtian production which was much criticised. A letter about it from Bergonzi was subsequently published in the *Opera* magazine. He considered that Wanamaker's production was "quite ruinous, his stupid movements not being in character with the score composed by our great Verdi. The scenic setting was similarly stupid because it was remote from realism; such 'imagination' is not acceptable to the true opera-lover".

I may not be a "true opera-lover" in Bergonzi's sense, but several Verdi productions I have seen have convinced me how wrong he was. I never saw Wanamaker's version, but the production of *La Forza* by Joachim Herz at the Komische Oper Berlin in 1975 was a riveting experience. The designs of Reinhart Zimmermann, based on seventeenth-century engravings surrounding the action, created a dark atmosphere in which the characters were driven by fate towards unwanted ends. With a very different approach, Jean-Pierre Ponnelle's highly stylised staging of *La Traviata* for the Opéra du Rhin in 1980 was able successfully to draw a physical and psychological barrier between the personal relationships of the principal characters and the superficialities of mid nineteenth-century salon society by placing the chorus of carousing partygoers behind a transparent wall, observing and commenting on the efforts of the courtesan heroine to find true love.

In my twenties, I enjoyed asking my friends to identify their Desert Island Discs, that is (à la Roy Plomley et alia) what eight recordings they would take with them if they were to be shipwrecked. The answers were always interesting and sometimes surprising; none more so than those given by Martin Schmid, whom I knew when we were both teaching at the University of Leicester. He was the son of Erich Schmid, the conductor of the Zurich Radio Orchestra, and had a sophisticated musical taste, so I was taken aback when one of his choices was an early Verdi opera. Why was he so impressed by what was, for me, "hurdy-gurdy Verdi"? He told me that he relished the cut and thrust, energy and directness of these works, simple though they may be.

Even if I might not put any early Verdi into my top eight, I was later to agree with Martin Schmid. What an evening at Reading in 1975 taught me was that this repertory is particularly well suited to younger performers. Operating on a shoestring budget with rudimentary sets in a hall more often used for degree ceremonies, the Reading University Opera offered *La Battaglia di Legnano*, a rarely heard patriotic piece about Italians defending themselves against foreign invaders. It must have stirred the passions of fervent Italian nationalists when it was first staged in 1849. Given by a predominantly student chorus and orchestra and by soloists at the beginning of their professional career, it was performed with such gusto and enthusiasm that it made no less an impact on us in the audience. There is something about the driving rhythms and lilting melodies in early Verdi that lends itself to performances off the beaten track, like that at Reading. The works do not come off so well in the glitter and luxury of the major international houses.

Rewarding experiences of this kind in unlikely venues constitute one of the real delights of opera-going. And Verdi has provided some notable examples. If I were to be asked which conductor of Verdi has given me most satisfaction, my answer would not be Carlo Maria Giulini or Claudio Abbado, though I have heard fine performances from both of these. I would pause before rejecting Edward Downes with whom I had some very good evenings at Covent Garden in the 1960s and 1970s and, presumably to the surprise of many, I would alight on Paul Daniel. He was Music Director of Opera North, in the 1990s and during this period gave superb interpretations of *Attila*, as well as *Trovatore, Luisa Miller* and *Falstaff*. To avoid the banality of oom-pa-pa, particularly in the earlier pieces, Verdi's scores require pliancy, careful phrasing and subtle accentuation, and Daniel's readings had all of these, as well as emotional thrust.

For many opera-goers, Puccini is chronologically the last of the composers that they regularly go to hear. Yet if this is the case, it is sad, suggesting that opera as an effective and popular art form ceased almost a century ago. It is true of course that, like other art forms, it suffered a crisis after the First World War, as modernism began to impact on composers.

As a young person so keen to relate to artistic creativity in the twentieth century, I did not want to believe that opera could not accommodate these developments. In terms of orchestral music, I had become very excited by Stravinsky, particularly *The Rite of Spring*, with its inventive, unexpected rhythms and highly profiled discords. It was with this work that I learned that "beauty" in music does not have to depend on traditional harmonic structures and that, in the right context and communicated in the right way, discords could be "beautiful". In a rather similar way, and at a similar period, I had discovered that the practice within jazz of playing off the beat was what made it interesting and exciting. So I was looking for an opera composer who could communicate through the language of twentieth-century music. Nothing radical, mind you, nothing too far from traditional tonality ... and I found the answer in Leoš Janáček.

The first experience was *Jenufa* at Covent Garden in 1969 with Rafael Kubelik as conductor, and at once I could respond to the idiom. This comprises, at times, jagged, repeated motifs in the orchestra operating, unlike their equivalent in Wagner, not as specific dramatic ideas but rather as capturing the general mood of the action or dialogue which it accompanies. At other times, there are rising lyrical phrases around which the vocal line soars in full-throated emotional outbursts. This combination of strikingly original harmonic and melodic effects, and of emotional intensity, carries the listener to the heart of the drama and makes for outstanding music theatre.

In my early opera-going days, Janáček was not well known, notwithstanding the pioneering performances at Sadlers Wells, conducted by Charles Mackerras. Within a decade or so that was all to change. First, in the 1970s, came a cycle of the major works shared by Welsh National Opera and Scottish Opera in remarkable productions by David Pountney with Maria Bjørnson as designer. Then, in the late 1980s, came an equally impressive cycle at Glyndebourne staged by Nikolaus Lehnhoff and Tobias Hoheisel and Janáček was now acknowledged as a leading composer of twentieth-century opera.

It cannot be said that he always chose easy subjects. *From the House of the Dead*, based on Dostoyevsky and set in a Siberian prison camp, contains mainly narrations by inmates of their past lives, while *The Makropoulos Case* is the story of a 300-year-old woman and of the legal complexities which attach to her continuing existence. Both need powerful productions which enable the audience to empathise with the leading characters and their fate, and the music can then do the rest.

Katya Kabanova is understandably more often performed. It involves a society with rigid social and moral codes from which the heroine seeks to be liberated. Although the conflict leads to dark tragedy, the humanity of her struggle shines through. *Jenufa* has somewhat similar themes and also provides some rich characterisation: the stepmother, the Kostelnička, prepared to kill a child to save the marriage of her daughter Jenufa; Jenufa herself whose child is the result of a passion for a lively but worthless young man (Steva) and who slowly, even grudgingly, finds eventual fulfilment through marrying his half-brother Laca; and Laca, resentful, morose, but loyal.

I have been to nine performances of *Jenufa* and only one of them failed to make an impact. Paradoxically this was when I saw the work close to Janáček's home territory, at the National Theatre in Prague. It was in 1976, a bleak time for the Czechs politically, and I had the impression that the grim realities of *Jenufa* had little appeal for them, hence a performance which treated it as if it were a folklore piece, in the manner of Smetana. This was hugely different from the expressionist interpretation given by the Welsh National Opera in a performance I had seen a year previously. I had taken with me a colleague who was a relative newcomer to opera, and I can still remember her outburst when the curtain came down at the end of the Second Act; I thought that she was going to burst with emotion.

A performance of the work at Brussels in 1991, conducted by Ingo Metzmacher, and with a superlative cast which included the veteran Wagnerian Anja Silja as the Kostelnička, so knocked me out that I was in a daze for an hour or so afterwards. When, the next day, I was on a train, I found myself by chance sitting opposite the Austrian tenor who had sung the role of Stewa. I felt bound to tell him that the performance had been *wunderschön* (very beautiful) but also *erschütternd* (shattering). Of course, he was pleased to get this reaction from me, but at the same time, also embarrassed, because when I approached him he was canoodling with a pretty young woman (his wife? A girlfriend? A lady from the chorus?) and in the circumstances would probably have preferred to remain anonymous.

Of the six composers listed at the beginning of this chapter, I come last to Georg Friedrich Handel, even though chronologically he is the first of them. There are two connected reasons for this: it is only within the last twenty years or so that Handel has come to be regarded as a major opera composer, and it was only during this period that I began to appreciate his qualities. In the 1960s and 1970s, staged performances of Handel's operas were rare. For one week each year, Sadlers Wells Theatre was occupied by the Handel Opera Society, led by the specialist conductor Charles Farncombe. Although sometimes famous singers (Joan Sutherland once appeared there) were engaged, the stagings were for financial reasons rudimentary and performances were largely supported by a faithful group of devotees.

Another pioneer was Alan Kitching who in the 1950s had converted the ruins of Abingdon Abbey into a small theatre. Over the next two decades he directed there small-scale performances of fifteen of Handel's operas which had not been performed in modern times. In 1975 this enterprise was moved to the Kenton Theatre at Henley where I saw *Lotario,* my first experience of Handel on the stage. It could have been my last! The plot was melodramatic and corny, the libretto, at least in its English translation, silly. The title role, written for a famous castrato, was performed by a counter-tenor who, though he sang well, was gawky in appearance and lacked acting skills. And the movement of the singers, surrounded by cardboard sets, was stilted and old-fashioned. But it was the musical structure which I most resisted, a seemingly endless chain of recitative and solo arias, all in the *da capo* form; that is, with three sections, the third being usually identical with the first, but coming after a contrasting middle passage. A whole evening of this I found tedious.

Today Handel's operas are widely performed, abroad as well as in Britain, and are well attended. My enthusiasm for them has now few bounds and I will travel many miles for a performance. How did all of this come about? To some extent, it was related to a growth in appreciation of baroque opera more generally, ranging from Monteverdi in the seventeenth century, through Lully and Rameau, to Gluck and early Mozart in the late eighteenth century. This interest was eventually to be fed by the increasing number of specialist singers and orchestra led by such conductors as William Christie, Christopher Hogwood and René Jacobs, performing what were claimed to be authentic versions of the score. But, initially at least, there was a reluctance to risk alienating audiences with the thinner sound and lower pitch of old instruments playing scholarly editions of early opera. Raymond Leppard, for example, had a huge success at Glyndebourne with his heavier, almost romantic, versions of works by Monteverdi and Cavalli.

Important also was the appearance of star, rather than specialist, singers. For me, indeed, the breakthrough in my struggle with Handel came in 1979 when the English National Opera production of *Julius Caesar,* conducted by Charles Mackerras, boasted Janet Baker as Caesar and Valerie Masterson as Cleopatra. I was still less than comfortable with what appeared to be the monotonous musical form, but was won over by the extraordinary singing of this famous pair. Something similar happened ten years later when, at the Royal Northern College of Music at Manchester, a young Amanda Roocroft, still then a student, conquered me and the audience alike with a brilliant rendering of the title role in *Alcina*.

Staging Handel opera poses problems for the director. As my Henley experience had proved, a realistic approach to production is doomed to failure because of the heavy reliance on solo arias. But what type of stylisation is appropriate? And how can this engage the audience's attention? Nicholas Hytner in his 1985 ENO production of *Xerxes* came up with an original and striking solution. He and his designer David Fielding were able to provide a visual equivalent to Handel's formal eighteenth-century approach by setting the piece in the Vauxhall Gardens of that period (see further, Chapter Nine). I was mightily impressed by the production when it was televised, but the impact was even greater when I eventually saw it at the Coliseum in 1992. It was nevertheless hard to tell whether what moved me most was Hytner's intellectual conceit, the elegant stage pictures of Fielding or the delectable Ann Murray in the title role.

A fear that audiences will too easily get bored by the structure of Handel's operas has led some directors to "over-produce" them, in the sense of having too much business on the stage. David McVicar was accused by critics of this when he mounted *Agrippina* for Brussels La Monnaie in 2000, a production which was later given at London's Coliseum and which I saw during its run at Frankfurt in 2006.

McVicar took a big gamble in offering a modern fashion-conscious setting for the story of a power struggle in the Roman Empire. However, few could object to the brilliant early scene when Agrippina followed her rival Poppea on the stage, wearing exactly the same elegant outfit, except that her heels were slightly higher. Later, having been outmanoeuvred by Agrippina, Poppea expresses her disappointment and anger in a sizzling aria. In this production she became a cabaret singer, drowning her sorrows at a glitzy bar, accompanied by a chain-smoking harpsichordist.

And the *da capo* repetitions of the aria were given a visual equivalent in the repeated movements of some tipsy dancers. Such effects nevertheless enhanced, rather then distorted, the music, and the audience were fully engaged in the drama, as well as being entertained. In my many operatic excursions in Germany, I have rarely sensed in those around me so much pleasure and enjoyment as at that evening in Frankfurt. At the end, they roared their approval.

The McVicar *Agrippina* was exceptional. My experience has been that efforts to "jazz up" Handel operas, or make them sexy, have mostly been distracting at best and vulgar at worst. Small scale, largely abstract, productions tend to work better. In Chapter Two, I described how a performance of *Tamerlano*, given in a studio theatre in the round, proved to be most effective. During the first decade of the twenty-first century the Dublin Opera Company brought several productions of this kind to the Buxton Festival with invariable success. This suggests that Handel's musical idiom has sufficient character and strength to communicate the drama without being reinforced by elaborate visual devices. I have the impression that, though it may take some time—perhaps half an hour or so—to "get into" a Handel opera, thereafter the music, combined with the drama, takes hold of one and does not release its grip until the very end. How and why is this?

I am not sure that I am able to find adequate answers to that question. A friend, who is a distinguished performer and educator, once surprised me with his explanation for my adoration of Handel: the music, he said, contains such great tunes. That might be so, but melodies are not necessarily conducive to dramatic characterisation. It is also the case that the orchestral writing is so often scintillating, carrying the listener forward with its dash and brilliance. But then how do we account for the fact that the slower arias are so moving, thus packing a quite different punch?

Perhaps it is simply that Handel had an intuitive gift for relating his own distinctive idiom to the demands of a (not always good) libretto, and that, as a result of his creative genius, insights on characters and their predicament emanate from the music. Then, as regards the apparently artificial structure of the operas, recitative and solo arias, the latter almost always adhering to the ABA model, we might actually derive satisfaction from awareness of how strict formal requirements are moulded—no, rather transcended—for the purposes of drama.

Of course, not all of Handel's operatic writing is at the highest level. There are plenty of *mauvais quarts d'heures*, particularly in the lesser-known works. It could hardly be otherwise, given his extraordinary output of some forty-five stage works, most of them written during a period of twenty or so years when he was also composing much church and instrumental music. I often have difficulty in distinguishing between the operas, not the least because almost all of them seem to have a single word title, nine of them beginning with the letter "A": *Agrippina, Amadigi, Alessandro, Admeto, Ariodante, Alcina, Atalanta,* and *Arminio*. But it is reassuring to realise that since, at the time of writing this, I have seen only twenty-one of the forty-five, there is so much still to discover.

Obviously I have been very selective in my six opera composers. What of the many others who feature in the repertory and who, over the years, have given me much pleasure?

I cannot overlook Monteverdi. Of the dozen or so operas that it is known that he wrote, only three have survived—*Orfeo, L'Incoronazione di Poppea,* and *Il Ritorno d'Ulisse*—and, given their extraordinary quality, it is maddening to realise what treasures must have been lost. *Ulisse* has a special poignancy for me. In June 1979, with Catherine, whom I was to marry a year later, I saw the Leppard/Hall production of it at Glyndebourne. Raymond Leppard's version, with a large orchestra and a heavier, more romantic sound, is today largely scorned by the cognoscenti, but we were overwhelmed by this *Ulisse*. It radiated warmth and emotion, as well as vitality and humour. Its heartrending climax was the long duet between Ulysses and Penelope when they were at last reunited, their voices intertwined in a celebration of love and fidelity.

Richard Stilwell and Frederica von Stade were the two marvellous singers and when Catherine died in 1998, it was their recording of the duet, made at Glyndebourne, which was played at her funeral.

I was a little slow to appreciate Rossini, perhaps because the vocal acrobatics which he demanded of his singers in their solo arias did not particularly appeal, and, to begin with, they captured my attention more than the brilliant, sizzling orchestral writing. Eventually I became more aware of, and was won over by, the latter, as also the witty and imaginative ensembles. In 1976 the La Scala Company gave a short season at Covent Garden and their *La Cenerentola*, conducted by Claudio Abbado in a production by Jean-Pierre Ponnelle, was a revelation. I can still remember the impact made by the famous sextet, towards the end of the opera, when the Prince and his valet turn up by surprise at the house where Don Magnifico, his daughters and Cinderella live. The basis of this passage is that each singer interjects into the ensemble a little florid phrase while the others repeat a steady rhythmic tune, rolling the "r"s in the phrase *"chi più sgrrrrrruppa più ragrrrrrruppa"*. As Lord Harewood says in his edition of Kobbé, it is one of the "high-water marks of comedy in music".

I have never seen Rossini's *Barber* in Seville, nor Wagner's *Meistersinger* in Nuremberg. I have, as it happens, seen Britten's *Death in Venice* at La Fenice in that city, but I take greatest pride in having been to Donizetti's *Emilia in Liverpool* on Merseyside, more specifically, in Liverpool's beautiful St George's Hall. In truth, this was not the greatest opera I have ever heard, but then Donizetti was hugely prolific and, unsurprisingly, among his seventy works for the stage there are some flops.

The best of his serious pieces are powerful, both musically and dramatically, while his comedies are witty and tuneful. Of the latter, the best known in this country are *L'Elisir d'Amore* and *Don Pasquale*, but my favourite, *Le convenienze ed inconvenienze teatrali,* has rarely been performed here. Perhaps the clumsy title—it literally means "The Conventions and Inconveniences of the Stage"—is partly responsible.

When I saw it in Freiburg in 1977 in a wonderfully funny production by Ulrich Melchinger, it was more engagingly called *Viva la Mamma*. It involves a send-up of opera itself, the mother in question (sung by a bass!) wanting to oust the prima donna from the limelight so that her soprano daughter might prosper.

As regards French opera, I have never been overwhelmed by *Carmen*. I confess to a weakness for Massenet, much as I have for marzipan: at the moment of consumption, I cannot get enough of it, but afterwards I feel a little guilty. *Pelléas et Mélisande* is another matter. It is unquestionably a masterpiece, Debussy's haunting score being so apt for the remote, mythical world created by the playwright Maeterlinck. If the vocal music is restrained, in comparison with what is typically experienced in more conventional operas, this seems so right for characters who have only an opaque identity and who are subdued by the oppressive environment in which they live.

The work made a terrific impact on me when I first saw it at Covent Garden in Václav Kašlik's 1969 production. This recreated its mystical, fantasy, quasi-medieval world through the designer Joseph Svoboda's use of lighting, projections and moving gauzes. But the claustrophobic atmosphere of the piece can be very effective in quite different settings and styles. The centrepiece in Harry Kupfer's production for the ENO in 1981 was a greenhouse in which the understated emotions of the characters became identified with hothouse plants. For the Opéra de Lyon's presentation at the Edinburgh Festival in 1985, Pierre Strosser set the piece in a *fin de siècle* chateau, its wealthy inhabitants being insulated from the real world outside. And for Opera North in 1995, Richard Jones and his designer, Antony McDonald, had the characters as expressionist contemporary figures playing out the drama, in costume, in a largely abstract setting. Each of these different stagings made for a very compelling evening.

In *Salome* and *Elektra,* his two early expressionist works written about the same time as *Pelléas*, Richard Strauss was stretching the boundaries of musical language, but after these striking contributions to twentieth-century opera he retreated into compositional conservatism. His lush, sometimes saccharine orchestration and melodious vocal writing, especially for sopranos, was to become somewhat anomalous for Germany in the 1930s and 1940s. When I was writing opera reviews for *Orpheus*, the Berlin opera magazine, I took a German student, who had been helping me with the language, to see the Glyndebourne touring production of *Capriccio*. This is a gentle, whimsical salon piece, largely concerned with the question whether words or music are more important in opera. The student found it incomprehensible, even shocking, that something like this could be written in Germany in 1942; and I could not disagree with her.

Alban Berg's two stage works, *Wozzeck* and *Lulu*, get much closer to what was happening, both politically and artistically, in Germany during this period. I have to admit that, hard as I have tried, I have never completely come to grips with *Lulu*. I can find little to empathise in the story of the decline and fall of a *femme fatale* which is told with a cool detachment. Nor am I much engaged by the music. The score was composed in accordance with the serialist technique, introduced first by Schoenberg, but it is not possible to perceive the twelve-tone structure simply by listening to the opera. Contrast this with, say, Handel and Wagner, where the relationship between the musical form used and the drama adds significantly to appreciation of the work.

Wozzeck, which Berg composed some years earlier with a much freer technique, is very different from *Lulu* and, in my experience, almost never fails to impress. This is partly because of the subject matter, and Berg's obvious compassion for those who are downtrodden and exploited in a harsh, militaristic society. But it is also because the musical idiom relates so well to that theme. For example, while tonality is used for the external world of military parades, tavern dancing and so on, atonal music explores the inner world of the characters and their obsessions. Nowhere is this better demonstrated than in the interlude between the two final scenes, after the crazed Wozzeck searches in the pool for the knife with which he has murdered his mistress, and then drowns himself. The orchestral sound builds on a chromatic chord to reach a mighty climax and then resolves itself into a nimble harmonic ending, as Wozzeck's child, unaware of what has happened, plays by himself "*hopp-hopp; hopp-hopp; hopp-hopp*". It is one of the most moving moments in all opera.

That Benjamin Britten, alone among post-World War Two composers, should have contributed several works to the mainstream operatic repertory is something for which we in Britain, once dismissively labelled by a German as *Land ohne Musik*, should doubtless be proud. And indeed, when I have seen Britten's operas abroad, notably *Peter Grimes* and the two comic pieces, *Albert Herring* and *A Midsummer Night's Dream*, I have been struck by the warmth of the audience's reception of them. Of course, Britten's music is much more approachable than that of most of his continental European contemporaries. Also *The Dream*, because it is a faithful adaptation of Shakespeare, has familiarity, while *Albert Herring* gains from being an example of *l' humeur anglais*, as well as giving foreigners a great opportunity to caricature the British. But *Peter Grimes* stands on its own feet, and remains as powerful a dramatic and musical portrayal of the outsider in a hostile society as it did when it was first performed in 1945.

My admiration for Britten's operas has always been tempered by some doubts. I find tiresome his obsession with boys' treble voices and also with the (presumably not unrelated) theme of doomed male innocence. At times, his music seems to be rather spineless, perhaps a consequence of his aversion to modernism. But unquestionably he deserves to be up there among the major opera composers even if he does not feature in my six "greats". And of all of those discussed in this chapter, he is the only one whom I have heard conducting one of his own works, *The Turn of the Screw*, given by the English Opera Group at Oxford in 1964. Not that this made much of an impact on me at the time, but it provides a nice link to the theme of my next chapter: performers…

CHAPTER EIGHT

PERFORMERS

Every two years, during one week of June, I spend (for me) an unusual amount of time in front of the television, watching, not tennis at Wimbledon, but the BBC Cardiff Singer of the Year competition. And, when I was working and living in Manchester, I regularly attended singing competitions at the Royal Northern College of Music. It is fun to compare one's own opinion with that of the expert judges who award the prizes. Often they seem to agree with my judgement; no, sorry, it should be the other way round: I agree with their judgement. But there have also been occasions when I have ground my teeth in irritation because a singer whom I thought was clearly the best was ousted by their choice.

Of course, we may disagree because we are looking for different qualities and, indeed, when judges of singing competitions discuss what they value most in performers, they come up with an amazingly diverse range of criteria. Some will mention the quality of the voice, others will stress technical prowess. Then there are dramatic skills: the ability to interpret the character of role and to communicate that character in musical terms to the listener. For some, this requires the singer to internalise the role so that he or she becomes that character; for others, it is important not to lose the sense of performance. Finally, there are judges who consider that all other aspects pale into insignificance compared to what they refer to as "star" quality, or the ability to get you to the edge of your seat with excitement.

I find it impossible to state categorically what, for me, are the most important qualities in a singer. In any event, what most impresses in a competition when performers are alone, in front of an orchestra or piano, is not necessarily the same as when they are integrated into a fully staged operatic production. For example, there is the question of how they move physically and how they interact with others in the cast. The individual performer I shall start with, and indeed chronologically my first "favourite" performer, is a case in point. The first entry in my opera *cahier*, the record of what I have seen, is Britten's *Midsummer Night's Dream* at Covent Garden in 1962, and in the cast list of singers, there is an asterisk against the name of Geraint Evans, indicating that I found something exceptional in his performance.

I doubt if all the characteristics which made this Welsh baritone such a great operatic performer would have fully emerged in a singing competition. He offered completely rounded interpretations of the characters he portrayed, and these were as much physical as vocal. I recall how, as Bottom in *The Dream* wearing an ass's head, he entertained his fellow rustics with a nimble donkey trot. By way of complete contrast, in another of his famous Shakespearian incarnations, as a corpulent Falstaff, he waddled around but was still able to retain a certain dignity in his wooing. There was something very alluring in his articulation of the Italian language, particularly in *buffo* parts, because it seemed to flow naturally from his strong Welsh accent with its melodious intonation. He is best remembered for his comic roles, but he was also an outstanding Wozzeck, anguished and sullen, when I saw that opera for the first time.

Geraint Evans was the first singer to be knighted while still performing since Charles Santley in the early twentieth century. He was also, in 1960, the first British singer to appear at La Scala since the 1920s. Indeed, unbelievable though it might now seem when British singers are well known around the world, they were, until Evans made the breakthrough, rarely invited abroad. Was this because it was perceived that their training prepared them better for oratorio than for opera? Or was it due to the fact that so many performances in Britain were given in English rather than in the original language?

Perhaps, and most unfairly, names had something to do with it. Would Maria Callas have had the same success if she had sung with her original surname Kalogeropoulou? There is a first-rate German conductor, Christoph Prick, who for understandable reasons has never made it in the anglophone opera world, though he has appeared there sometimes under the name of Christoph Perick.

We know that, in the first half of the twentieth century, British dancers like Lilian Marks had to adopt Russian-sounding names (Alicia Markova) to be taken seriously. Some singers from the English-speaking world have likewise wanted to give the impression that they were Italians. In 1995 I was in Hamburg for a lacklustre performance of *Rigoletto*. I did not realise at the time that Mario di Marco, who was disappointing in the title role, was not Italian but Irish, and had been a member of the Sadlers Wells Company in the 1970s, when he was known as Niall Murray. Perhaps he should have learned something from the fate of Donald Pilley, whom I heard in 1966 as a very promising young tenor singing Rodolfo in *La Bohème*. A year or so later, a disc came out with a recording of some Verdi pieces sung by Donaldo Pilli. However, his career never seemed thereafter to take off. The American tenor Stephen Algie may have done better when he became Stefano Algieri. In any event, Sir Geraint did very well staying as Evans.

Towards the end of his singing career, Geraint Evans was invited to direct a few opera productions including, at the Edinburgh Festival in 1976, *The Marriage of Figaro*. The prospect was, for me, enticing, since Evans was to sing Figaro opposite the Count of Dietrich Fischer-Dieskau, another of my favourite singers, and Teresa Berganza was to be Cherubino, with Daniel Barenboim, still then primarily a pianist, conducting. In truth, although Fischer-Dieskau gave an excellent performance, it was not a great evening. During the interval I bumped into an Oxford colleague and his terse comment was, "Well, it's a singer's production".

He meant by this that Evans had not attempted to impose on his colleagues any overriding interpretation, but had allowed them to explore their own ideas about their roles. As we will see in the next chapter, this approach to opera production was, in the late 1970s, gradually being replaced by one in which directors sought to integrate individual performers into their own, sometimes novel, conception of a work. But, particularly in the larger theatres where companies engage international star singers on a short-term basis—the *stagione* system— the traditional approach, epitomised by the Edinburgh *Figaro,* was still frequently encountered.

Now I might say, along with other old fogies, that "they don't have opera singers like they used to". But this statement needs some explanation. It is not because the quality of opera singers has declined in the past forty years; on the contrary, I believe that the average quality has improved. Rather it is because in the "good old days" star singers stood out more than they do today. Opera production was often then less an integrated dramatic affair and more an environment in which singers performed. It is said that before the Second World War some famous singers were not willing to attend a rehearsal but would send their dresser to get the necessary information from the "stage manager" as to where they should stand and move. I doubt if this ever happened in my time as an opera-goer but I recall some performers who showed a relative lack of interest in what was going on around them.

A classic case was Carlo Bergonzi. He was one of the leading tenors of his generation and at the height of his powers when I saw him as Manrico in Verdi's *Il Trovatore* in 1965. This role is usually taken by a *tenore robusto*, a singer with a large, powerful voice but often little grace and sensitivity. Bergonzi was different. In Act Three he was certainly capable of meeting the demands of the martial air *Di quella pira*, with its notorious high C, but immediately before it he had enchanted us with his refined interpretation of *Ah, si ben mio*, bringing to that aria great delicacy and sweetness of tone. We cheered him, of course, overlooking the fact that he was visually an implausible hero, ambling about the stage in a rather purposeless way.

Singers could stand out simply because of the quality of their voices, sometimes beautiful, sometimes large, sometimes both. This was particularly true of Italianate tenors who could get away with murder, in terms of artistic endeavours, as long as the public could enjoy their brilliant upper register. Pavarotti may have become one such case, but when I heard him early in his career, as Alfredo in *La Traviata,* he made a smaller, more elegant, sound. In contrast, I remember, sitting in the remoter sections of the Amphitheatre at Covent Garden and being knocked back by the stentorian tones of the somewhat lesser known Renato Cioni. He was singing the relatively short role of Gabriele Adorno in *Simon Boccanegra* and, no doubt aware that he did not have to pace himself, he let fly in the aria *Sento avampar nell'anima.* A huge bass voice can also make a great impact. Although these seem to have emerged mostly from Russia or other East European countries, my favourite was that of the Finn Martti Talvela. His large physical frame and massive sonorous vocal capacities were equally imposing.

Big female voices are the exception rather than the rule and you do not want them, for the sake of power, to sacrifice colour and intonation. Under pressure, a *forte* can turn into a screech. But listening to a soprano who can maintain quality and a rounded tone at full power can be an exhilarating experience. Unquestionably, this was true of Birgit Nilsson. I have already described, in Chapter Five, how I and the rest of the audience in Munich were bowled over when she sang the Dyer's Wife, opposite Fischer-Dieskau, in *Die Frau ohne Schatten.* This was in 1977 and she was then nearly sixty years old, but the opulent, golden sound soared into the auditorium.

Yet it would do Nilsson an injustice to suggest that sound and volume alone made her an outstanding performer. She had great interpretive skills, able to adjust her phrasing and timbre to the character of individual roles. So when she was Turandot, the gleaming upper reaches of the voice remained cold and aloof. In the role of Elektra, it had an aggressive, even hysterical, edge. And when I was fortunate enough to hear her Brünnhilde in the *Ring* at Bayreuth, it was striking how vocally she was able to develop the character. It started as the impetuous young goddess of *Die Walküre* (a carefree *Ho-jo-to-ho* trilled upwards). In *Siegfried* there was the slow sexual awakening (a restrained, less open sound as she was made aware of female vulnerability—*Ich bin ohne Schutz und Schirm*). In *Götterdämmerung*, when betrayed by Siegfried and vowing vengeance, there was venom in the voice, but when all had to be resolved in the final Immolation scene, it broadened into full-throated ecstasy.

Birgit Nilsson enjoyed having fun and she may well have needed this after hours of serious Wagner singing. Those who have seen the BBC documentary of the recording of the Culshaw/Solti *Ring* in Vienna will remember how, during a run-through of the Immolation scene, just at the moment when Brünnhilde summons Grane her horse to join her in self-sacrifice, a real horse trotted on from the wings. Nilsson's face dissolved into laughter at the joke.

Most of the singers, like Birgit Nilsson, who made a big impression on me during the first decade of my opera-going combined vocal qualities and interpretive skills. Take Mirella Freni. Apparently, when a baby in Modena, she shared the same wet nurse as Pavarotti and is reported to have claimed that he must have got all the milk! Maybe, but she had a lovely creamy voice which suited so well the role of Micaëla in *Carmen* which I heard her sing in 1970. She was able to invest the aria "*Je dis que rien ne m'épouvante*" with such touching simplicity and sincerity that she won all hearts. It is said that when Herbert von Karajan was conducting a performance of this in Salzburg, he just leaned on the podium and indicated to the orchestra to follow Freni.

The career of the great Swedish tenor Nicolai Gedda was remarkable in several ways: he started off as a bank clerk; he mastered, and could sing in, seven different languages; and he continued performing professionally well into old age. In 1997 at Covent Garden I was there for his last stage appearance, singing a cameo role in Pfitzner's opera *Palestrina* when he was seventy-one . He was in very good voice and, needless to say, we cheered him to the echo. It brought back memories of when I had heard him thirty years previously. Covent Garden had decided to mount, for the first time, Berlioz's heroic work *Benvenuto Cellini* and he was the obvious choice for the title role. Not only did he have the voice, steely yet tender, used in impeccable idiomatic French, but he also had the ability to differentiate musically between Cellini as an artist seeking glory and Cellini as an ardent lover.

It is nevertheless wrong to assume that voices have to be beautiful to make an impact. That of Peter Pears, for example, had a dry, white quality, bordering on falsetto. It could also be mannered in delivery, an aspect brilliantly satirised by Dudley Moore in the sketch *Little Miss Muffett* in *Beyond the Fringe*. At the same time, the unusual timbre gave it a haunting character which was most effective dramatically. His last great role was Aschenbach in Britten's *Death in Venice*. A few months after the work's premiere at the Maltings Snape, the English Opera Group brought it to Covent Garden. Britten had been careful to restrict the volume of the orchestral accompaniment to Pears' solos, so that they sounded more like *lieder* than opera. But it meant that the singer was able, in this much larger theatre, to project his musings on Aschenbach's moral and physical decline with the emotional engagement which he and Britten brought to their famous recording of Schubert's song cycle *Die Winterreise*.

It was interesting that Pears and the Canadian tenor Jon Vickers both sang the title role in *Peter Grimes* with great success, but their voices and interpretation could hardly have been more different. While Pears was a dreamer, Vickers, with his massive rugged and masculine voice, was a brute. He did not make a lyrical Italianate sound and was, therefore, more suited to the German repertory. Listening to recordings of him, one may recoil because the size of the voice combined with its penetrating character can grate, but these very characteristics worked very well in the theatre because of the intensity of Vickers' delivery. I recall, when I saw him as Florestan in my first *Fidelio* at Covent Garden, how at the beginning of Act Three his first piercing utterance *"Gott"* in the aria *"Gott! Welch Dunkel hier"* filled the darkness of the stage and the auditorium before we could see him. And, needless to add, he was a heart-rending, impassioned Tristan when he came, eventually to sing that role late in his career.

My final category of outstanding performers from this period is that of singer-actors, those artists who combined vocal prowess with considerable dramatic gifts. There was none finer than Tito Gobbi, the leading Italian baritone of his generation. His preparation for each role which he undertook was meticulous in its attention to detail. For example, when working on the part of Schaunard in *La Bohème*, he was puzzled by an aspect of the Act One scenario. Schaunard, the musician, has had more success than his fellow students, and made some money from working for an eccentric Englishman. So he has bought some food for all of them. But why, wondered Gobbi, does he blather on for some time about the Englishman, not seeming to notice that his hungry friends are already stuffing themselves? He came up with the answer that Schaunard must have been short-sighted and that his glasses had steamed up when he entered the attic.

Luckily for me, Gobbi was a frequent visitor to Covent Garden. His Iago, which I saw in 1968, may have been, by modern standards, a conventional interpretation of evil, but with sinuous movements of the body and eyes, accompanied by delicate *mezza voce* as he imitated Desdemona, his provocation of Othello into jealousy was masterly. He is perhaps best remembered for his Scarpia in *Tosca*. Because he made the character refined, elegant, even attractive, the cruelty and sadism became even more frightening. This portrayal, which I saw at Covent Garden in 1966, had the excellent Marie Collier in the title role, but when Franco Zeffirelli's production had originally been mounted two years previously, Gobbi had played opposite Maria Callas (whom alas I never heard live). And during that run of performances, an incident, curiously related to the Schaunard business, occurred. Callas was very short-sighted and had not noticed how close her costume was to a pair of lighted candles and she set fire to her wig. Gobbi decided that in the circumstances he should attempt to embrace her before this was justified by the libretto and by doing so was able to smother the fire in her hair. His hand was burnt, but without his intervention, things might have been far worse, worthy of inclusion in my Chapter Four as a real calamity.

Tito Gobbi was the brother-in-law of the Bulgarian bass Boris Christoff, though it is difficult to credit this, given the animosity between the two great singers. Christoff was a temperamental artist and not an easy man to work with. A member of the Covent Garden chorus, being interviewed on his retirement, proudly recalled that Christoff once spoke to him. When asked what the star singer had said, the chorister replied, "He said, 'Get out of the way!'".

Be that as it may, Boris Christoff was a wonderful singer-actor. In 1966 I saw him in what are, perhaps, the two greatest operatic roles written for basses, Boris in *Boris Godunov* and Philip in *Don Carlos*. What impressed me most in both performances was the contrast, physical and vocal, between the public and private persona of these two rulers. When he made his first entrance as the Tsar he had a majestic presence but, at the same time, by movement of his eyes, indicated his awareness and apprehension of the crowd around him. As the Spanish king, his physical demeanour, stern but vulnerable, was perfectly matched by the vocal expression, a large dark voice which rang out when necessary but which held the audience in a spell in the quieter passages, as he communicated his anxieties and loneliness.

So, was this a Golden Age for opera singers? Was it the case, as I have suggested, that performances stood out because at that time stage directors allowed singers more freedom to offer their own interpretation of their roles? Another possibility, and one that I would not too quickly dismiss, is that the general quality of acting-singing has significantly improved and that therefore there is less of a distance than there once was between star performers and average performers. My own impression is that standards in, for example, provincial and fringe opera companies have risen considerably during my lifetime.

I have to admit also that there may be a simpler, autobiographical explanation for the prominence of the 1960s and early 1970s in my memory of great singers. The proportion of performances involving international stars I attend at Covent Garden and elsewhere has been, for many years, much smaller than in that earlier period. One reason is that I have lived much further away from London. Another is that I have derived much pleasure from operatic excursions into the unfamiliar, in terms both of repertory—famous singers are generally not interested in singing obscure pieces—and of opera houses—smaller theatres cannot pay for international stars.

Nevertheless, a list of the famous singers I have heard live since 1975 is a long one and I can hardly ignore all of these. At the top of that list is Placido Domingo. Amazingly still, at the age of seventy-one, singing major roles, he is rightly regarded as a phenomenon. Not allowing himself to be seduced by the razzamatazz of "The Three Tenors" or commercial dumbing-down, he has throughout his long career preserved artistic integrity. Blessed with a natural handsome voice, he sings with style and intelligence. The music director of the New York Met, James Levine, is reputed to have remarked to him once, after a performance of *Tosca*, that he had "the brain of a conductor", to which Domingo's response was: "It's a good thing you don't have the mind of a tenor".

Translating from the Spanish, Domingo's name means "Quiet Sunday". But this is belied by his stage performances, which are very committed. He had already acquired this reputation in 1975 when I was eagerly anticipating my first live experience of him at Covent Garden as Riccardo in *Un Ballo in Maschera*. I was disappointed. His characterisation of the role was thin—he was not helped by the dull, conventional production by Otto Schenk—and he was not in his best voice. Happily, when I saw him two years later as Johnson in *La Fanciulla del West*, it was a completely different story. My review of the performance for the Berlin magazine *Orpheus* was, I now admit, embarrassingly cliché-ridden, but it captured my enthusiasm. "Domingo", I wrote, "was simply breathtaking. He identified himself completely with the role … The richness and expressive quality of his voice, combined with the ardour of his performance, won the hearts of the audience."

Perhaps the most remarkable feature of Placido Domingo's career has been his versatility, and his willingness to explore new territory. From his earlier successes in the lyrical tenor repertory, he moved into the heavier, more dramatic roles, for example, Otello, and then, more controversially, even Wagnerian roles (Siegmund, Parsifal, Tristan). Finally, when the upper register began to show signs of wear, he took on some baritone roles, notably Simon Boccanegra.

As the Germans would say, Domingo thus ventured well beyond his original *Fach*. This is a nice little word meaning field of study and, when used in relation to singers indicates the type of voice and appropriate repertory (heldentenor, buffo bass and so on). When pronounced correctly, with the "a" sounding as an English "u", it comes uncomfortably close to the most famous Anglo-Saxon four letter word. I admit, therefore, to have been initially much taken aback when, one evening at a formal dinner at Oxford, an American woman next to me asked "What is your *Fach*?" Perhaps I should have replied, "Madam, this is neither the time nor the place … "

There is little so frustrating as travelling to hear a star, only to find that that person is a pale reflection of what he or she had been, as experienced in a recording. In 1994, I drove some fifty miles or so to Düsseldorf for *Der fliegende Holländer,* the cast including Peter Meven, a famous Wagnerian bass who had sung at Bayreuth and at many of the world's leading opera houses. It is sad to report that he came adrift during the performance. It was unclear whether this was because he had lost his voice or because he had missed an entry; but his confidence was gone and he could barely be heard for the rest of the evening. He did not appear at the end for a curtain call and I learned subsequently that he had retired from the stage.

In contrast, what a joy to hear young singers at the beginning of their career when it is obvious that they are going on to bigger and better things. In the last chapter, I mentioned that the only time that Janáček's *Jenufa* has failed to make an impact on me was, paradoxically, when in 1976 I heard it in Czechoslovakia, the composer's own country. But that performance had a compensating feature, a young soprano in the title role. She had a luscious, warm voice, ideal for the lyrical passages, but also with sufficient colour to characterise the spectrum of emotions from despair through doubt to hope. Her name was Gabriela Beňačková. She was then twenty-nine and unknown in the West. It came as no surprise that two years later she was engaged by the Vienna Staatsoper and was soon thereafter to become one of their star singers.

In 1998 a German colleague, knowing of my taste for Wagner, invited me to visit him in Kassel and there to see *Siegfried*, given by the local company. He admitted that he was rather apprehensive as to whether the performance would be good enough for me. This was understandable: Kassel is a relatively small town and putting on one of Wagner's major works is an ambitious undertaking. Good Wagnerian singers are hard to come by these days and casting *Siegfried* is particularly problematic because a heldentenor capable of doing justice to the title role is indeed a rare beast. And when Siegfried made his entry early in Act One, on trotted a little chubby chap, an appearance far removed from one's expectations of the mythical hero. Yet he sang beautifully, with a lyricism that much of the part demands but rarely gets; and he also had sufficient steel in his voice to ride the orchestra in the forging of the sword.

"What did you think of our Siegfried, Christian Franz?" asked my friend. I replied that he was one of the best I had heard. Although only thirty at the time, astonishingly young for such roles, the following year he was engaged to sing them in Berlin, and subsequently at Vienna, Bayreuth and the Met. I encountered him again at Cologne and Hamburg and he never failed to impress. Interestingly, too, the fact that he had an amiable stage personality and was no tall, blond Aryan archetype meant that directors had to adapt their interpretation of the character of

Siegfried to his appearance. Given the unpleasantness of the original, this may not have been such a bad thing!

While I was delighted to have "discovered" Beňačková and Franz, the case of the Lancastrian soprano Amanda Roocroft was a little different. Her performance as Fiordiligi in *Cosi Fan Tutte* at the Royal Northern College of Music, in 1998, when she was a student and only twenty-one, had drawn lavish praise from the veteran critic Michael Kennedy: "For sheer potential, at this stage of her development, I have not heard [her] equal. If ever I heard and saw star quality, this was it". So, when, a year later, I was at the College for its annual opera production, I expected something special from her appearance in title role in Handel's *Alcina*. I was not disappointed: she gave a dazzling interpretation, both vocally and dramatically. But, one has to ask, was it wise of Mr Kennedy to impose on a student singer the burden of such plaudits? What a responsibility it must have been for her, in the years which followed, to live up to a reputation created by his language.

Sadly, it is far from unusual for the career of promising young singers to founder because they rocket to fame and cannot cope with the pressure, or rush to take on roles for which they are not yet ready. Take the case of Linda Esther Gray. She had impressed when I heard her in 1973 as the Countess in *Figaro* with the Glyndebourne Touring Company: a fine voice with a good stage presence. It was felt that she had the potential for heavier roles, and when I next saw her, ten years later, she was Kundry in the Welsh National Opera's *Parsifal*, conducted by Reginald Goodall. Clearly, by then, she was going places. The voice had deepened and gained in strength, fully matching the demands of the part, and she had the Wagnerian intonation, enabling her to bring psychological meaning to the text. Indeed, within the next year or so, she was singing at Covent Garden and Paris, and elsewhere abroad. There were also plans for her debuts at La Scala and the New York Met, but these were not to materialise. Preparing to sing Turandot for Scottish Opera, she had a crisis of confidence in her vocal technique, from which she never recovered. Her career was effectively at an end.

In the days when singers were members of a permanent ensemble and would work their way to the top, starting with smaller roles and building their career more slowly, this kind of problem was rarely encountered. Even without institutional constraints, some singers, no doubt under the wise guidance of their teachers or coaches, move only gradually from lighter to heavier roles and in consequence have greater lasting power. At a performance of *Simon Boccanegra* given by the Welsh National Opera in 1970, I was struck by the imposing singing and stage presence of the Paolo, the secondary baritone role in the piece. The same singer, Thomas Allen by name, turned up the following year in the company's *Magic Flute* as Papageno, costumed as a Red Indian, but delivering the text, and dropping in a few comic asides, in a Wearside accent. It was a brilliant performance.

In the following years I was to hear him in several Britten operas. He was a swaggering self-confident Sid in *Albert Herring*, a lively Ned Keene in *Peter Grimes*, and a fresh-voiced and alarmingly innocent Billy Budd. In 1977, at Covent Garden, he brought the house down with his rendering of the famous aria *"Avant de quitter ces lieux"* in Gounod's *Faust*, and that when he was in the stellar company of Alfredo Kraus, Mirella Freni and Nicolai Ghiaurov. Yes, Allen had made the big time, and was now a considerable artist, but he had reached that position through steady progress, a strategy which was to pay off, since at the time of writing this, over thirty years later, he is still singing in major opera houses.

In 1984, I was a Professor at Newcastle University and a member of the Honorary Degrees Committee there. Given Thomas Allen's connection with the North-East—he was brought up in Seaham in County Durham—I proposed that he should be honoured by the University. My proposal was accepted and I could not have been more pleased when the Vice-Chancellor asked me and Catherine to look after Tom and his wife during the day of the degree ceremony. As far as he was concerned, the occasion was not entirely problem-free because, fitting the visit into a busy schedule, he found himself in Newcastle without his luggage and he had to go out and buy himself a new suit. But, for us, it was most enjoyable: he was so warm, friendly and unassuming. Catherine could later recount with pride how she had been kissed by one of the world's great Don Giovannis, and I was to meet Tom several times again after performances, enabling us to exchange opera gossip and for me to learn something of the opera world from the inside.

Thomas Allen received a knighthood in 1999, a worthy reward for his dedication and services to opera. Some singers whom I have greatly admired have not always received the recognition which is their due— my "unsung" if not "unsinging" heroes. I have in mind artists who, though they may not be in the top international bracket, can be relied on to throw themselves completely into their assigned roles and give a committed performance. An excellent example is the Yorkshire tenor Paul Nilon. His career began slowly, and in the 1980s I heard him only in minor or supporting roles. Then, late in that decade, he took the tenor lead in some Mozart operas, including the *Magic Flute* with the City of Birmingham Touring Opera and *La Finta Giardiniera* with Opera North. I remember being struck by the clarity and elegance of his singing and his acting skills. But that did not really prepare me for what was to come.

Paul Nilon's voice acquired greater weight and the range of his repertoire expanded. When, as happily occurs from time to time, Opera North enterprisingly stages a rare opera with a juicy tenor role, it is as likely as not to call on him. In 1990 it had given us the British premièrepremière of Carl Nielsen's fine comedy *Maskarade*, in which Nilon was an amusing and sweetly-singing hero. He was mightily convincing in 2011 as the painter who sacrifices art for money and fame in another UK premièrepremière, *The Portrait* by the Polish-Russian composer Mieczyslaw Weinberg. But the never-to-be-forgotten highlight was in 1997 when Opera North mounted *Julietta* by Bohuslav Martinů. This is a surrealist work in which we follow the central character, a French bookseller, through his dreams. Nilon's performance of the role was a tour de force. In the *Opera* magazine Max Loppert wrote of him:

"Always a singing-actor brave, truthful, flexible and original in outlook, he has found in the opera's long, demanding central role an unsurpassable vehicle for his multifaceted theatrical and musical talents".

Now this might suggest that, contrary to my earlier observation, Nilon's abilities were sufficiently recognised. But reviews like this did not, it seems, lead to appearances at the major opera houses—well, with one or two exceptions. In 1996 I obtained a returned ticket for the revival at Glyndebourne of Rossini's *Ermione* which had been given its British premièrepremière there the previous year. The well-known Mexican, Jorge Lopez-Yanes, was due to return for the role of Pyrrus, but he had cancelled and Paul Nilon, who had been engaged for the subsidiary part of Pilades, was elevated to the tenor lead. Now, Rossini's arias for this voice include some stratospherically high notes and they are generally performed by specialists in this repertory, like Lopez-Yanes. Nilon is not such a specialist, but he did not flinch from the demands of the part and was musically satisfying throughout. What earned him the ovation at the end was, however, his characterisation of the seedy, lecherous Pyrrus, an interpretation which was much more powerful than that of Lopez-Yanes which has been preserved in the DVD of the production.

From Chapter Four you will know something of the frustrations caused when singers cancel, but also that substitutes can be surprisingly good and thereby provide some compensation. There have, of course, been many cases of artists launching their international career after being called on to replace celebrities who cancel at a late stage. I cited the example of the German soprano Marlis Petersen, who twice stepped in when the French star Natalie Dessay pulled out. A performance I recall with much pleasure was that of the young Russian, Marina Poplavskaya, who in 2009 at the Hamburg State Opera gave a stunning account of Violetta in *La Traviata* when Elena Mosuc inexplicably became unavailable. At Covent Garden, Poplavskaya had leaped to fame by stepping in at short notice to replace perhaps the two most acclaimed sopranos of the day, Anna Netrebko and Angela Gheorghiu, the former as Donna Anna in *Don Giovanni*, the latter as Elizabeth in *Don Carlos*.

The "substitute" singer who lives most vividly in my memory also had a role in *Don Carlos*, though this was in Frankfurt in 2007. The American tenor Andrew Richards, who was to have sung the title role, had cried off a few weeks before the first night of David McVicar's new production. The substitute, Yonghoon Lee, was making his European debut—indeed, had barely completed his vocal training—but he gave a magnificent performance. Possessing a powerful tenor voice which gleamed like steel in the sun, he also was a master of Verdian phrasing and acted the part with energy and conviction. It was no surprise to learn that he was later to succeed Jonas Kaufmann in the same role at the New York Met.

Marina Poplavskaya is from Eastern Europe—as are Anna Netrebko and Angela Gheorghiu. There is nothing new in great singers coming from this part of the world. Think of the De Reszke brothers, Chaliapin, Maria Jeritza, and many, many others. But in recent years, no doubt aided by the fall of the Iron Curtain, and relaxed labour migration controls, there has been a veritable invasion of the West by singers from countries such as Russia, the Ukraine, Bulgaria and Poland.

Eastern Europe is relatively close and contains a huge population. South Korea, the homeland of Yonghoon Lee, is in contrast a single, distant country with a population of under fifty million. Yet, quite astonishingly, opera companies, particularly those in Germany and Austria, rely heavily, for soloists as well as chorus, on Korean singers. Whether this has something to do with the climate in Korea, the national temperament or the quality of vocal training, it is difficult to tell. Whatever the explanation, the teaching establishments in Seoul produce a seemingly endless stream of talent for what must be, for them, a foreign culture.

The number of South Koreans who may be considered international stars is still rather small—I would place the soprano Sumi Jo and the bass Kwangchul Youn in that category. Irreverently, I wonder if this has something to do with their names many of which, to Western eyes and ears, may appear to be only too similar. For example, the Operabase list of current professional opera soloists reveals that, alongside Yonghoon, there are seventy-five other Korean singers with the surname "Lee", while for "Kim", if you work your way through from Ah Yun Kim to Wookjung Kim, you find well over one hundred. I am reminded of the predicament of the rugby commentator trying to distinguish between the eight "Jones" in the 2008 Welsh Grand Slam squad. And, staying in that part of the world, it should not be forgotten that Bryn Terfel Jones dropped the last part of his name so as not to be confused with the Welsh baritone of an earlier generation, Delme Bryn-Jones.

East European singers have been particularly prominent in those Italian and French operas which require big voices; less so in German works, perhaps because hitherto their training has not focused on this repertory. The South Koreans, who tend to be smaller in physical frame, have generally lighter voices, ideal for Mozart and bel canto roles. But one should resist stereotyping this as their vocal *Fach*. While I have not heard of a Korean Brünnhilde or Tristan, I appreciated Kwangchul Youn as an excellent Gurnemanz at Bayreuth and his compatriot, Antonio— not presumably his original name—Yang was a first-rate Alberich in Lübeck.

Indeed, it has sometimes been agreeable for my expectations regarding national characteristics to be confounded. If I may have expected most female Australian sopranos to be big, bold and brassy, what a pleasure it was to encounter the elegant, even aristocratic, Yvonne Minton who touched the hearts of all as, for example, the Composer in Covent Garden's 1976 production of *Ariadne auf Naxos*. And need I remind you of the sleek and seductive Danielle de Niese from whose more recent appearances my eyes would not turn, when she was Poppea at Glyndebourne and Ginevra in Handel's *Ariodante* at Paris.

Conversely, at least until the 1980s, British singers did not have a reputation for having big voices. Rather, like Stafford Dean, Elizabeth Harwood and Marie McLaughlin, they were best known abroad for their interpretations of Mozart. British tenors were, on the whole, characterised as having thin, reedy instruments, incapable of meeting the demands of the heavier, more glamorous Italian roles, let alone Wagner. But in recent times, when heldentenors are few and far between, I have heard the Cornishman John Treleaven as Tristan in Frankfurt and Londoner Christopher Ventris as Parsifal in Bayreuth. Both gave sterling performances and the pleasure of the stereotyped expectation being upset was—forgive me—tinged with a sense of national pride.

In my earlier opera-going days, Italian singers, particularly tenors, had a reputation for being hammy actors, raising and dropping their arms in time with the music, and playing to the gallery. I suspect that, at the time, their training focussed almost exclusively on the voice, and dramatic technique was neglected. Things changed somewhat in the 1980s when I came across, at Glyndebourne, Max-René Cosotti and Ugo Benelli. Both were admirably lithe and engaging on the stage, while at the same time singing with a fresh, sensitive tone. Admittedly, both were specialists in Mozart and Rossini and, for the next two decades, I continued to experience problems of wooden and clichéd performances from Italian tenors in the heavier Verdi roles. Then, at last, in the 2000s, I encountered Marcello Giordani, Giuseppe Sabbatini and Giuseppe Filianoti, each of them refusing to conform to the caricature of Italian tenors; rather, giving subtle dramatic interpretations without losing the gleaming sounds for which their predecessors were most famous.

You will have gathered from the last paragraphs that I have a marked dislike for singers who do nothing more on the opera stage than show off their voices. I am even more irritated if they indulge in the awful habit of milking applause. A generally effective means of doing this is to insert an unauthorised *ritardando,* slowing down just before the final note or phrase of aria, thus signalling to the audience that something special is about to happen. Ugh!

While I am about it, what other practices make me squirm? Well, I do not like it when singers are far too obviously keeping their eyes glued to the conductor's beat, thus completely dispelling any dramatic illusion that they are trying to make. If, for example, the hero is engaged in a passionate embrace with the heroine, it does not enhance plausibility if he has to swing her around so as to view the baton and make sure that his exultant *"Io t'amo"* comes in on time. Admittedly, this is encountered less frequently these days simply because in most opera houses there are television monitors spread around the pit and the stage, so that singers can see the conductor from almost any angle or perspective.

Then there is the matter of prompting. Now, the prompter in the little semi-circular box immediately beyond the footlights—*trou de souffleur* in France, *Souffleurkasten* in Germany, but simply *buca* in Italy— is a familiar feature of traditional opera houses. The prompter often acts as a secondary conductor, relaying the beat or otherwise helping the singers. Normally this is done unobtrusively, although in a piece such as Donizetti's *Le convenienze ed inconvenienze teatrali*, which is actually about an opera being performed, it can be used to great effect in the production, normally as part of the comic business. And it is not unknown for a singer, while taking applause at the end, to bend down and shake the hand of the prompter.

Sometimes, particularly when singers are less than fully confident in their part, the prompter's role is more elaborate. To aid their memory, singers are given the opening words of each line a few seconds before these are to be sung. If you are close to the stage, you can sometimes hear the prompt and, needless to say, it is very distracting. Of course, if a singer has been called in at the eleventh hour, perhaps to replace another who is ill, it is understandable and, indeed, a small price to pay, if the alternative is singing from a rostrum from the side of the stage, or worse still, cancelling the performance. But where singers are, or should be, familiar with their roles, it is irritating because it inhibits dramatic spontaneity. I can recall a performance of *Siegfried* given by English National Opera in 1979 at Sunderland—yes, difficult as it is now to believe, the whole of the *Ring* was in that year given in Sunderland—when the singers performing the three leading male roles, Siegfried, Mime and The Wanderer, all had to be prompted throughout the evening. To put it mildly, this was disconcerting, particularly when there was a dialogue between two of them: it was as though there was a conversation going on nearby.

Clearly conductors are "performers" in one sense, but I am not clear that I want them to be so in all senses. It is not unusual for conductors to engage in acrobatics when they are directing an orchestral concert and, on the rostrum, are in full view of the audience. It happens less often when they are half concealed in the theatre pit. In 2010, I was in Amsterdam for *Turandot* conducted by Yannick Nézet-Séguin, a young French-Canadian, who had established a reputation of being one of the most exciting talents in the business. His prancing around was a distraction even though it was in the pit, and it provoked in me ill humour rather than admiration, not the least because, from time to time, there seemed to be a lack of coordination between orchestra and singers. In other words, for all his passion and showmanship, Nézet-Séguin had not got the basics right.

This is not to imply that I am suspicious of energetic conductors. In my earlier opera-going days, Georg Solti at Covent Garden was a real hero, particularly in Wagner. He was physically active in the pit—indeed, Richard Strauss once asked him why he "thrashed around so" when conducting. But there was control and overall design, as well as passion. Solti was appointed as Musical Director of the Royal Opera House at a time when foreign conductors were respected by the Establishment, but British conductors were not. This attitude may have provoked the mischievous question from Thomas Beecham, "Why do we employ so many third-rate foreign conductors in this country when there are so many second-rate English ones to choose from?" But the attitude and his remark were most unfair, and of course there have been many excellent British conductors of opera in the period since, including Colin Davis, Edward Downes, Mark Elder and Richard Armstrong, to name but a few.

As I revealed in Chapter Seven, one of my own favourites has been Paul Daniel, particularly when in charge of a Verdi performance. Another is the insufficiently noticed Elgar Howarth who excels in twentieth-century music. That this is unsurprising is not so much because of his first name. Rather, he was a fellow student at Manchester in the 1950s of that extraordinary group of musicians, Harrison Birtwistle, Alexander Goehr, Peter Maxwell Davies and John Ogdon, all of whom contributed so much to contemporary music in Britain. Howarth was responsible for the memorable UK premièrepremière of *Maskarade* I have already referred to. More significantly, perhaps, he was able to convince me, for the first time, that Birtwistle could actually write alluring and compelling music for the stage. He conducted the world premièrepremière of *The Second Mrs Kong* at Glyndebourne and I heard it when the production was subsequently on tour.

Even less well known is the Welsh conductor Wyn Davies, but if, at the beginning of a comic opera by, say, Rossini or Offenbach, it is a little bespectacled man with a white pointed beard and a broad grin who steps into the pit, you can be sure that you are in for a good evening, musically. The performance will be full of wit and sparkle.

At the 1997 Pesaro Festival the principal event was a staging of Rossini's grand opera *Moïse et Pharon* in the huge Pala sports arena. The impressive production—an updating to the fate of the Jews in the twentieth century—was by Britain's celebrated Graham Vick. I found it surprising that the musical direction had been entrusted to a twenty-five-year-old Russian, Vladimir Jurowski. But his command of the large forces was assured, and there was a compelling dramatic impulse in his interpretation of the score. A year later I was in Berlin, at the Komische Oper, where I heard two Russian works: Prokofiev's *Love of the Three Oranges* and Rimsky-Korsakov's *Tale of Tsar Sultan*. The excellent conductor of both was also Jurowski, but Mikhail who, it turned out, was Vladimir's dad.

We know very well that music talent often runs in the family—think of the innumerable Bachs—and fathers and sons who are opera conductors, active at the same time, are not that unusual. For example there were Armin (who died in 2006) and Philippe Jordan in Switzerland, and in

France there are Michel and Emmanuel Plasson. But then in Antwerp in 2009, for a performance of Tchaikovsky's *Mazeppa*, I encountered yet another Jurowski in the pit. This was Dmitri, Mikhail's other son and Vladimir's brother, and predictably it was a powerful and satisfying performance. Mikhail's father, another Vladimir, was incidentally a composer. I am only sorry that I have not come across his daughter, Maria, who is a music teacher.

As I noted in Chapter Four, Pierre Boulez once famously remarked that he thought that all opera houses should be burned down. That was at the time of the student revolution, in the late 1960s, when radical criticism of bourgeois art was all the rage and when Boulez was better known as an avant-garde composer than as a conductor. Yet, notwithstanding this revolutionary call to arms, I have heard him conduct some magnificent performances in opera houses including, in 1969, *Pelléas et Mélisande* at Covent Garden. From my experience of him in the concert hall, particularly when conducting contemporary music, I expected clarity and a resistance to slushy, wishy-washy sounds which emanate from some Debussy interpretations. I got both of these but in addition there was what I did not expect, a powerful impulse which made the opera a drama of real people, rather than one of fey, dreamy characters. So also, in 2007, when giving at the age of eighty-two what he claimed would be his last performances of opera, *From the House of the Dead*, at the Aix-en-Provence festival, Boulez injected such emotion into the dissonances of Janáček's score, that we shared in the pain of the prison camp inmates. At the end, the tumultuous applause which greeted his solo bow was such as nearly to bring down the new Grand Théâtre de Provence—and that would have been an irony, given his remarks of forty years previously.

Have I experienced great conducting at the other end of the age spectrum? Well, I have to admit that when, in 1975, I went to see Glyndebourne's touring production of *The Rake's Progress*, with David Hockney's brilliant designs, I felt that there was something special about the musical interpretation. Stravinsky's pastiche of baroque music was wittily realised, particularly its sprightly rhythms and odd harmonies. In the pit was a twenty-year-old with a shock of hair—his name was Simon Rattle.

I was to hear him twice more at Glyndebourne, in Haydn and Prokofiev, composers both obviously suited to his talents. But then, many years later, at the Salzburg Festival in 1999, came a real surprise. He was then, of course, internationally famous but was not known to have any interest in French baroque music which is a turn-on more for early music specialists. However, there he was, billed to conduct *Les Boréades* by Rameau. In truth, the performance had little of the arcane gentility that one tends to associate with authentic early music performances, but that was because Rattle hurried the music along at a great lick and it made for a scintillating evening. He was aided by the showbiz production of Karl-Ernst Herrmann, the soloists and chorus tapping their feet to the syncopated rhythms.

What happened on the stage was of little help to Simon Rattle when I had my last outing with him in 2011. It was *Der Rosenkavalier* in Amsterdam, the production of which was old-fashioned and tedious. But this was not all: as I have recounted in Chapter Four, Lady Rattle (Magdalena Kožená), who was to have been the Octavian, had cancelled a few weeks previously; and the major part of Baron Ochs had to be sung from the wings. With the disappointments on the stage, my eyes kept roaming towards the pit from which most characterful sounds emerged. There was nothing clichéd about the waltzes which were sharply defined, as were the witty interjections of the woodwind. Comedy indeed, but Rattle was also capable of shading the orchestration in the quieter, more introspective moments, or else letting loose with lyrical ardour when this was called for. Afterwards my young companion said to me, "Sometimes you realise that star performers *can* give you something special". "Yes", I replied, "sometimes … "

CHAPTER NINE

PRODUCTIONS

In November 2008 I was in Northern Germany, and Wagner's early opera *Rienzi* was being performed in Bremen. *Rienzi* has some good moments but it is a long (it would play for about seven hours if uncut) and predominantly tedious work. I had, however, seen an imaginative small-scale production of it mounted by a young Nicholas Hytner for the English National Opera in 1983. Moreover the Bremen production was to be directed by Katharina Wagner, the composer's great-granddaughter. So I attended the performance; or more precisely two-thirds of it, as I left during the second interval. It was a total disaster, quite the worse Wagner production I have ever seen.

Rienzi is the story of a medieval Italian dictator who succeeds in outwitting the aristocracy to attain political power on behalf of the general populace, only eventually to be abandoned by them. Unsurprisingly, directors have drawn parallels with twentieth-century political figures; Hytner's production was based on the rise and fall of Mussolini. In Germany, some sensitivity on the issue must be expected. It is said that Hitler saw the work in his early years and was influenced by it. Katharina Wagner's method of addressing the problem was to debunk the notion of a political hero by turning the opera into a farce.

The "hero", on his first appearance in front of the Romans, was bald. So (to charm them?) he went to a hair salon to try on a variety of wigs, eventually choosing a blonde one with pigtails. In another scene, he entered with a vacuum cleaner strapped to his back, and soldiers in his army were similarly "equipped". At the battle scene, he rolled around half-naked in pools of red paint. What dramatic insights could we gain from incidents like these? None at all; it was all too puerile; and, apart from anything else, ugly to look at and clumsy. I said all of this in a letter I subsequently wrote to the Intendant at the Bremen theatre, finishing with the phrase "God help Bayreuth!" This was a reference to the recent announcement that Katharina Wagner was, jointly with her half-sister Eva, to take over artistic direction of the Bayreuth Festival.

As it happened, I was at the Bayreuth Festival some nine months later. Fortunately, I did not have tickets for Katharina's version of *Die Meistersinger* which, by all accounts, was just as bad as her *Rienzi*. Rather, I was able to see *Parsifal* mounted by the Norwegian director Stefan Herheim. I was not entirely without forebodings since, although the production had received good reviews, it was also an attempt to "deconstruct" the work; and, to say the least, my experience of "deconstructions" had not been altogether happy. Herheim sought to apply the central ideas of *Parsifal*, birth, death and redemption, to the history of modern Germany and indeed to the role of Bayreuth within it. So the innocent hero is seen growing up in Villa Wahnfried, the Bayreuth home of the Wagner family, and the Festspielhaus itself becomes the Hall of the Grail with, at one moment, a huge mirror descending to show that we the audience are part of the history.

Parsifal is "born" into bourgeois, late nineteenth-century Germany, and then he experiences in turn militarism and fascism. Kundry, in the original a wild, wandering woman harassed for mocking Christ on the cross, is portrayed as a Jew. Towards the end, the meeting of the brotherhood of the Grail takes place in the German Federal parliament in the 1950s, but it remains ambiguous whether the innocent hero is able to secure redemption for this unhappy gathering.

Apart from one episode (the flower maidens transformed into First World War nurses entertaining wounded soldiers with razzamatazz) which was in bad taste and said nothing dramatically, this was a penetrating and ultimately very moving approach; and it had intellectual coherence. It was also beautiful to look at, the designers Heike Scheele and Gesine Völlm creating impressive representations of the lofty comfort of Wilhemine Germany, but also the strident aggressive images of the Third Reich. Technically the production was able to move smoothly from one setting to another, aided by video projections which set the atmosphere without being over-intrusive. The scenography was successful, above all, because the visual images flowed with the music.

The extremes of the ridiculous in Bremen and the sublime in Bayreuth well reflect the vicissitudes that one finds in modern opera production. Back in the 1960s when I began opera-going, it was unheard of for directors to approach mainstream works in the way described. So what has happened? And why?

Those whose experiences of opera do not date back that far will find it hard to believe how old-fashioned many of the stagings were in the 1960s. That was certainly true of Covent Garden. To some extent it was a consequence of keeping productions of the more popular operas in the repertory for a long time and wheeling them out for visiting stars. What creativity or imagination there may have been when the production was first mounted soon disappeared as the original director rarely returned for the revival. It was left to the "house" director to work through, with the cast, appropriate movements on the stage—and invariably these were conventional. Nor did it help that the shabby decor might be from a bygone age.

In 1976, there was a revival of Verdi's *Macbeth* for which a fine cast had been assembled: Sherrill Milnes in the title role, alongside Grace Bumbry, Franco Tagliavini and Robert Lloyd. But, my goodness, what a pathetic production: stock melodramatic gestures in front of cardboardy sets. It seemed to be all the more absurd because half a mile away, at the Aldwych Theatre, Nicol Williamson and Helen Mirren were generating huge electrical excitement in Trevor Nunn's unconventional production of the play for the Royal Shakespeare Company.

Now it may have been the case that, in those days, opera managements were reluctant to impose innovatory approaches on international star singers. I recall a production by Renzo Giacchieri of another Verdi piece, *Ernani,* at Rome in 1978 which contained some interesting ideas. The chorus, for example, engaged in some stylised movements and a sombrely dressed mime figure followed the villain of the piece whenever he appeared on stage—perhaps it was his dark soul. But the principal singers behaved as if they were performing in any conventional staging, coming up to the footlights, singing their arias with arms gesticulating, and completely ignoring what was happening around them. It was as though the director had created the production without the soloists and, when they arrived, he had just let them do their own thing within its framework.

This is not to condemn all stagings during this period. While the vast majority were traditional, mainly realistic, presentations of what the composer and librettist intended, some were powerful dramatically and beautiful to look at. That was the case with Luchino Visconti's famous *Don Carlos* for Covent Garden—the production which effectively "rediscovered" for British audiences this wonderful piece—and also with the many stagings there of Italian opera for which Franco Zeffirelli was both director and designer. So, for example, in his *Cavalleria Rusticana* you could almost feel the heat of the midday sun beating down on the Sicilian village and the torrid emotions which it fuelled there.

Zeffirelli was fond of spectacle, particularly as he grew older, and some of his later productions seemed to concentrate on this to the detriment of drama. Now, of course, there is a long-standing association between opera and spectacle and for many opera-goers it is important. The huge popularity of the big-scale productions at the Verona Arena or Caracalla Baths in Rome—*Aida* with horses, chariots, and perhaps even elephants—testifies to this. And I myself was not always resistant to enjoyment of this kind. My first experience of Wagner was *Die Meistersinger* in 1963. I am now ashamed to admit that what made the biggest impact on me at the time was not the intimate musing of Hans Sachs on life and art, nor the beautiful quintet. Rather it was the last final scene when the Covent Garden stage was filled with the different guilds assembled to jolly tunes and dancing.

Two years later, the Royal Opera House decided ambitiously to mount the British première of Schoenberg's impressive but difficult opera *Moses und Aron*. The director Peter Hall, better known then for his innovative and penetrating Shakespearian productions, perhaps wisely, perhaps because he was under some pressure to do so, went for spectacle. The news then got around that for the climax of the piece— the Dance around the Golden Calf and the ensuing orgy—the stage was filled with 300 singers and extras, two horses, one donkey, one cow and six goats and, most enticing of all, twelve striptease artists hired from a Soho agency to play the naked virgins. No wonder that, for this very modern piece, all seats were quickly sold.

In the 1960s and early 1970s, there was a general reluctance to abandon realism in the staging of opera. This was understandable, at least as regards the international companies, since productions of the repertory operas typically had to last for a number of years and several revivals, employing a variety of singers. The newcomers would be familiar with what was expected of them if the work was mounted in a traditional way, and therefore could slot easily into an existing production.

Nevertheless, to avoid dull routine, some directors sought to inject novelty into this approach and one possibility was to change the period in which the opera was set. The updating of opera is so common today, original period settings having become the exception rather than the rule, that it is difficult to appreciate how innovative this was forty years ago. In 1976, when I saw on tour a revival of the 1973 Glyndebourne production of *Capriccio* by Richard Strauss, with a young Felicity Lott in the pivotal role of the Countess, it came as a pleasant surprise that the director John Cox and his designer Dennis Lennox had chosen to set it in the 1920s, rather than the eighteenth century. *Capriccio* is a whimsical salon piece and the elegant nonchalance of the twenties was both appropriate and engaging. The secret of this production's success lay in the fact that an audience of the 1970s could relate much better to the manners and style of the chosen period than they could to something two hundred or so years old.

Puccini's operas have benefited from this approach. For example, transposing the setting of *Tosca* from Rome in 1800 to 1940 and turning Scarpia into a nasty henchman of Mussolini can hardly fail to make an impact. My own favourite Puccini updating was Phyllida Lloyd's *La Bohème* for Opera North, first staged in 1993. In Anthony Ward's superb designs, the Paris of the 1830s became Paris in the late 1950s, with motorbikes, images of James Dean, French abstract painting and a general atmosphere of Left Bank (and left-wing) student life. These images resonated with us, if only from films we had seen of the period, and added poignancy to the romances of the Bohemians.

Updating also allows the audience to enjoy the ingenuity with which a director can transfer the original to the idiom of a different period. Perhaps the most famous example is Jonathan Miller's production of *Rigoletto* for the English National Opera. Sixteenth-century Mantua was transposed to New York's Little Italy in the 1960s and the Duke of Mantua to the "Duke" of a mafia gang. The most irresistible moment was when, waiting for his tryst with Maddalena in Sparafucile's bar, the Duke pops a coin into a juke box and out comes the rum-ti-tum accompaniment to the famous aria *"La donna e mobile"* which he then sings. An equivalent gag occurred in John Dew's 2004 production of *Die Walküre* at Wiesbaden. In a mid-twentieth-century setting, the Valkyrie warrior maidens were commanders in Wotan's "air force" and for their "Ride" they were stationed in an air traffic control centre, so that they could bellow their *"Hojotoho! Heiaha"* into the intercom.

Often the transposition is made to the period when the opera was written. This enables the audience to think about the relevance of the story to the society with which the composer and librettist would have been familiar and therefore to themes which may have inspired the work. It is not, for example, unusual for some of Verdi's works which contain power struggles, such as *Il Trovatore*, to be given nineteenth-century settings. Although his own involvement in the Italian nationalist movement was at the time ambiguous, he was in his later life identified with it, and earlier pieces such as the Chorus of Hebrew Slaves in *Nabucco* were assumed to have had a political subtext.

The case for adopting this approach becomes even stronger when a piece clearly reflects the composer's own period rather than the one in which it is ostensibly set. A good example is Gounod's *Faust*. This is a musical adaptation of Goethe's dramatic poem, the basis of which was medieval legend. With its trite and sentimental contrasting of good and evil, Gounod's version does little justice to Goethe's philosophical essay, emerging more as an expression of Victorian morality and religion. This was beautifully reflected in Ian Judge's 1985 production of the work for English National Opera and subsequently Opera North. The crowd surrounding Marguerite to condemn her sexual misbehaviour were stern gentlemen dressed in black and wearing top hats. And Faust, a priest, dabbling in black magic, quitted the real world to engage in dangerously immoral fantasy.

Sadly, updating is also frequently used when the director has little or no faith in the dramatic value of the libretto and wants, for the sake of the music, to liven it up. This seems to happen most frequently with comic operas, presumably because it is felt that the original is too corny or at least insufficiently funny. In my experience, Rossini has had to suffer this treatment far too often with silly, vulgar transpositions that are too coarse for his brilliantly witty and sprightly music.

But for sheer awfulness I cannot remember a worse example than that of Scottish Opera's production of *Oberon*, a rarely performed piece by Weber. Admittedly the libretto is a pretty rum affair with its combination of knights in armour, Arabian princes and fairies, but it has some fine music. To "rescue" it, Anthony Burgess was commissioned to write a completely new text and he obliged by turning the chivalrous heroes into American airmen and the Arabian prince into an Ayatollah. That hardly solved the problem of the fairies, so the director Graham Vick decided to have the drama set in a cinema where everybody could pretend that it was a children's tale. And of course the whole thing became a vulgar farce, as well as a mish-mash.

Spectacle and/or excessive attention to realistic detail can often distract from the core of a drama. The celebrated director Peter Brook, who had cut his teeth mounting productions at Covent Garden in the 1940s, wrote at length on this in his book *The Empty Space*. And when he returned briefly to opera in the 1980s, it was to offer a small-scale version of *Carmen* in his modest Parisian theatre Les Bouffes du Nord. The experience of this production was for me novel but not entirely successful. One problem was that the music of *La Tragédie de Carmen*, as Brook had renamed it, had been pared down to fit the physical dimensions of the theatre. I was not entirely convinced that the inner drama of the piece was sufficiently compelling without the colour and weight of the original orchestral score and the extravagance of a full-scale production.

Baroque opera lends itself more to the small-scale approach. This is partly because of the smaller orchestra required for these earlier works, but partly also because their dramatic content tends to depend less on specific locations and therefore on decor. This was brought home to me in unusual circumstances. In 1981, I was on a day trip to Milwaukee, and when in this characterful, but not beautiful town, I saw to my astonishment notices indicating that Monteverdi's *Coronation of Poppea* was to be given that evening. I may be forgiven for not having had high expectations of a performance of this seventeenth-century piece in the American Midwest. The company responsible for it was called the Skylight Comic Opera and, I assumed, would be comfortable with, say, Gilbert and Sullivan or Offenbach, rather than Italian baroque. Nor was it reassuring to find that the theatre was a small performing space above a coffee shop.

In fact, this performance turned out to be the operatic highlight of six months spent in the USA, far surpassing what I saw at the New York Met and in Chicago. With a few props and adroit use of the limited space, the director Stephen Wadsworth was able, through movement and gesture, to get his singers to communicate the passions, jealousies, and thirst for power which dominate Monteverdi's amoral drama. This was, apparently, the first opera that Wadsworth had directed. No surprise that he was soon to leave behind the Milwaukee attic and move on to bigger things with productions at the Met, La Scala, the Vienna Staatsoper and Covent Garden. Nor that the company was to change its name to the Skylight Music Theater.

The intimacy of the Skylight theatre facilitated the Brook-style "empty stage" approach. The closeness of the audience to the performers meant that it was almost impossible not to get fully involved with the characters and the relationships between them. And a production of this kind need not be visually dull. In the autumn of 2011, the English Touring Opera performed Handel's opera *Flavio* in a number of smaller theatres. The designer, Joanna Parker, had coloured the plain walls surrounding the action in a dark blue. This, combined with the varying and subtle lighting effects created by Kevin Treacy, beautifully captured the mood of the drama and heightened the emotional impact of the music.

That the "empty stage" approach can be equally effective in a larger, more conventional theatre was borne out by my experience of *Le Nozze di Figaro* in Brussels in 1998. This was my fourteenth *Figaro*, but certainly the most original and most satisfying of all of them. Usually the opera is given a realistic production, whether in its original eighteenth-century setting, or in some updated equivalent, the class struggle being played out against a decorated, luxurious background of evident wealth. Here, however, the decor surrounding a mainly empty stage consisted simply of bare, somewhat decaying, walls and two large double doors. The costumes were a mixture of modern and period and, as a further indication that this was "theatre", the stage curtain was drawn backwards and forwards to reveal the different scenes.

A blog which I found on the Internet complained that Christof Loy, the director, and Hubert Murauer, his designer, had "emptied the work of its nobility". But that was surely the point: the predicament of the characters and their relationships could be felt all the more powerfully by us in the audience precisely because we could concentrate on them without the distraction of pretty pictures.

The Brussels *Figaro* would have been too radical for the 1960s and 1970s and yet even then there had been some movement towards more abstract productions. Perhaps the key figure was Wieland Wagner, the composer's grandson. He and his brother Wolfgang had resurrected the Bayreuth Festival after the Second World War and had had the difficult task of denazifying it, given its close association with Hitler and the Third Reich. This political necessity was combined with an artistic endeavour to link the performance of opera to its roots in Greek theatre, and that implied concentrating on the inner drama, bringing out particularly its psychology; and getting rid of all the romantic stage clutter of traditional Wagner productions. So, for example, Wieland's abstract staging of *Die Meistersinger von Nürnberg* was dubbed by its critics as *"Die Meistersinger ohne Nürnberg"* ("The Mastersingers without Nuremberg") and was clearly very different from the spectacle which I had so enjoyed at Covent Garden.

As I have recorded in earlier chapters, as a young man in the throes of Wagnermania, I made my first visit to Bayreuth in 1967 to see Wieland's third production of the *Ring* there. Tragically, he had died the previous year but one of his protégés had taken responsibility for the revival and the production had changed little. The action took place on an almost bare stage, surrounded by large blocks incorporating often ancient archetypal images, reminiscent of Henry Moore's sculptures, but not of Nordic mythology which was the inspiration for Wagner's original drama. Much use was made of lighting effects, setting varying moods or picking out individual characters. The singers were mainly static, so that their slightest physical movement acquired major dramatic significance.

Reflecting on all of this afterwards, I could see how the production had offered a powerful psychological interpretation of the *Ring*: Wieland was known to have been interested in, and influenced by, Jungian and Freudian theory, and a programme note indicated how he saw the work as a conflict between the male and female principles of life and of different facets to these basic categories. But, I confess that, at the time, I missed images of the dragon, of the forest, of the castle and of fire and water; and found the abstraction unrelentingly severe.

Today I look back at my 1967 Bayreuth experience with a mixture of ruefulness and nostalgia. I have been subjected, particularly in Germany, to such perverse interpretations of Wagner and other operatic masterpieces and to so much clutter and frantic and unnecessary movement on the stage that I have come to yearn for the purity, sobriety and intelligence evident in Wieland Wagner's production.

Many people enjoy opera precisely because, with its heroes and villains and its romances from bygone ages, it is remote from the wearying concerns of everyday life. As is the case for nineteenth-century ballet, some works in the repertory can be presented as fairy tales, with pretty, colourful pictures providing pleasure to accompany the music. Mozart's *Magic Flute* frequently receives this treatment and invariably with success. The same applies to several pieces by Rimsky-Korsakov. I recall with great affection *Christmas Eve* which in 1988 was mounted by the English National Opera. Sue Blane, who some years previously had been responsible for the costumes in David Pountney's exotic staging of Rimsky-Korsakov's better-known *Golden Cockerel*, here created an extraordinary toytown Russian village with, in the opening scene, a devil and a witch flying over the roofs. It seemed to come straight out of a Chagall painting.

The same approach has worked very well for some early baroque comic operas drawing on classical legends and involving interplay between the gods and mortals. Francesco Cavalli, whose works were only rediscovered in the 1970s, provides some good examples. Herbert Wernicke's 1993 production of *La Calisto* at Brussels was so remarkable that I went back to see it when it was revived there in 1996. The set was a box with, on the walls, painted allegorical representations of heavenly constellations. The mortals entered through a trapdoor, while the gods descended from the skies on chariots. Visually dazzling, the production reached its climax at the end, the stage darkening while the heroine ascended to take her place among the twinkling stars.

The fairy-tale approach does not necessarily have to be associated with escapism; it can have a serious, even bitter, edge to it. Take, for example, the 2008 production of Dvorak's *Rusalka* at Grange Park. With its bright colours and fantastical costumes, Antony McDonald's designs could have come straight out of the pages of a picture book. It is the story of a wood nymph who is transformed into a human to follow the prince whom she loves, but it ends tragically when she cannot cope with the "real" world. McDonald convincingly found in it a gripping commentary on the dangers of relationships built on romantic illusions. Perhaps the most striking scene was that in which, to move from fairyland to the world of mortals, Rusalka's beautiful fish tail was surgically severed, so that she emerged from the operation with a pair of blood-stained legs.

I was in my twenties when I began to rebel against realistic opera productions. I do not think that it was a coincidence that, at the time, I was becoming more appreciative of early twentieth-century art. I realised how artists were able to communicate what they felt about the subject matter of a painting by distorting aspects of it, whether perspective, outline or colour. Stage designers could, of course, do the same thing.

One example was Maria Bjørnson who with David Pountney mounted in the 1970s a Janáček cycle for Scottish Opera and the Welsh National Opera. *The Makropoulos Case* tends to be less popular than the other operas, perhaps because its plot is a curious one. It contains a complex and apparently unending lawsuit and a woman who has taken an elixir and lives for over 300 years. Bjørnson created for the First Act, set in a lawyer's office, a multi-tiered, enormous range of bookshelves which totally dominated the stage. So we could relate this visual image to the themes of the work: fusty, old-fashioned ways of doing things; lives being organised by dry, complicated documents and procedures far removed from the vitality of human beings and their emotions—and, beyond this, whether immortality really is an attractive proposition.

Using unnatural colours, or exaggerating the movements or the personalities of performers so that they become caricatures, can intensify the emotional content of a piece. This expressionist approach is ideal for Alban Berg's *Wozzeck* and was superbly realised in a production of it which I saw in Nancy in 2006. The downtrodden central figure of Wozzeck was the only "realistic", three-dimensional, human being; around him were parodies, some of them grotesque, of an unfeeling society. But it was above all the colours which matched perfectly Berg's powerful score. The sky, for example, turned from blue through violet to a deep crimson red, when, as the sun set, Wozzeck murdered his mistress and filled the auditorium with cries of "Blut". Strange that this performance should be given in France, rather than Germany, the home of expressionism. But the director's name was appropriately Michel Deutsch and he hailed from Strasbourg on the French-German border; so perhaps that explains it.

It was, by coincidence, in Strasbourg that some years earlier I became aware of the power of stylisation, that is, where the production avoids a literal depiction of the action and instead imposes some form or pattern which conveys to the spectator the essence of the work. It was in 1977 and the opera in question was Verdi's *La Traviata*. Even today, this piece is most often given a realistic treatment because its highly specific setting—mid-nineteenth-century France—and its dramatic detail both lend themselves well to a traditionally devised spectacle in the Zeffirelli mould.

But Jean-Pierre Ponnelle, who was responsible for the Opéra du Rhin production, decided that a conventional lavish pictorial approach was too banal for a piece which was essentially about the loneliness of the courtesan heroine Violetta. So, when the curtain went up, and we heard the quiet slow opening notes of the prelude, we saw her alone on a dark stage. With the help of a candle, she groped around eventually, as the famous tune surged up in the orchestra, finding her own corpse under a table. And, in Act One, the partygoers, instead of ambling around the salon and flirting as they downed glasses of champagne, stood behind a transparent screen, observing and commenting on Violetta, as though they were members of a chorus in a Greek tragedy.

Stylisation can be used in variety of ways. As regards design, that which lingers most in my memory is the Glyndebourne 1975 production of *The Rake's Progress*, which subsequently toured the world with great success. It is not difficult to understand why: David Hockney came up with a brilliant solution to how Stravinsky's neo-classical pastiche, based on the Hogarth paintings, could be visually reinterpreted. Stravinsky had used formal devices—arias and the like—and a limited range of vocal and orchestral sounds to reflect an eighteenth-century style, but yet invested the score with ironic, modern harmonies. So, to mirror this, Hockney's sets were full of symmetric patterns and mainly black-and-white, which set off some touches of colour in the costumes. And on the backdrop were satirical drawings and slogans, bringing out the morality of the piece.

There can hardly have been a better example of visual presentation matching musical idiom than Hockney's *Rake*, but in its different way a production I saw of *The Barber of Seville* in Prague in 1976 was almost as good. What the director, Ladislav Stros, and his designer, Květoslav Bubenik, did was to link this famous comic opera to its roots in the Italian tradition of *commedia dell'arte*. This was a stylised form of theatre in which stock characters, such as Harlequin, Columbine and Pantalone, satirised human behaviour through caricature and energetic, often improvised, action.

The framework worked extremely well for the *Barber*, since its plot involves wily servants outwitting doddering old fools, as well as courtship through disguises, both of which were central to the *commedia dell'arte* tradition. Admittedly I may have been particularly appreciative of the visual dimension to this production, because *Lazebník Sevillský* was sung in Czech and I could understand nothing of the text.

To be effective, stylisation must communicate something of the piece to the audience and that is, I fear, the problem with the work of Robert Wilson, the current opera director who makes the greatest use of this approach. When I first attended one of his productions, *Die Frau ohne Schatten* at the Opéra Bastille, I was impressed by the abstract setting which reminded me somewhat of Wieland Wagner, and the blue and green lighting effects. But I could make nothing of the strange, ritual hand gestures of the singers, nor of their slow progressions across the stage, apparently disregarding all that was happening around them. Although these movements may have matched the musical rhythm, they had no obvious connection with anything in the text. When in subsequent Wilson productions of *Das Rheingold* and Bach's *St John Passion*, also in Paris, the very same features reappeared, I became bored and irritated.

The 1976 Bayreuth centenary production of Wagner's *Ring* was bravely assigned to the French theatre director Patrice Chéreau; aged 32, he had previously staged only one opera. At first, Chéreau's approach was greeted with much critical hostility but, by the time I saw the televised version which was broadcast some years later, it had been recognised as a major breakthrough in opera production and, in many quarters, acclaimed as such. The controversy it had originally generated was, I suspect, not so much because Chéreau had taken an overtly political interpretation of the work. That was by no means novel—George Bernard Shaw in his book *The Perfect Wagnerite* had seen *The Ring* as a parable on the follies of capitalism. Rather, audiences had been upset and confused by the fact that the work was set in a multitude of different periods. For example, in *Rheingold* some of the gods were in baroque costume; in *Die Walküre* Wotan wore a Victorian tailcoat; and in *Götterdämmerung* Siegfried, while holding a sword aloft, appeared in a dinner-jacket.

As we have seen, opera-goers had come to accept that productions might be set in a period different from that envisaged in the libretto, but what was the point in mixing up periods, thereby sacrificing coherence and plausibility? Now, if this question had been put to Patrice Chéreau and (unlike most directors) he had been prepared to explain his approach, I suspect that his response would have been something like the following. A dramatic purpose is served by destroying the illusion that those on the stage are reproducing what happens in real life. Spectators should be made aware that this is theatre, and that the opera in question has something to say to them which transcends any particular time or place.

That might be the theory; but whether or not "deconstructing" a work in this way makes for an effective and satisfying performance in the opera house is another matter. My very mixed experiences with the approach suggest that much depends on how well the presentation serves the music, whether it can avoid excessive complexity and thereby incomprehensibility, and whether it is attractive to look at, or at least provides an interesting spectacle for the audience.

For a production which scored highly on all of these points, there can be no better example than Nicholas Hytner's version of *Xerxes* for the English National Opera. Originally mounted in 1985, I saw it in 1992 and such has been the success of the show that it was still being performed at the Coliseum in 2005 and San Francisco in 2011. The Handel opera, which concerns the amorous adventures of the Persian conqueror, was set in the Vauxhall pleasure gardens in the eighteenth century. Visitors strolled around, observing displays of pieces of antiquity, but would stop to listen as the protagonists in the drama sang their arias, expressing their feelings on love, duty, power. It was, if you like, a visual counterpart to Handel's baroque exploration of classical virtues and vices.

But Hytner and his designer David Fielding also introduced into the proceedings some deliberate anachronisms; for example, the visitors sat down in modern deckchairs. We thus were not allowed to seek refuge in the belief that this was simply an eighteenth-century pageant. It was something relevant to us and our times. And even those who might refuse to draw out these inferences would nevertheless find irresistible the elegance and wit with which the production was executed.

At the other extreme from Hytner's *Xerxes* was a production of *Il Trovatore* which I saw at the Deutsche Oper Berlin in 2004. The performance was on a Saturday evening and I was puzzled to find that the theatre was only two-thirds full, and this for one of Verdi's most popular operas, with a strong international cast. As the performance began to unfold, I soon understood why. As Leonora sang her First Act aria about her love for a mysterious troubadour, there descended from the flies a huge photo of a swarthy youth, naked apart from a tattoo on each arm and a black tape covering his private parts. A hooded executioner then appeared and displayed, in front of the photo, a guitar and a human skull. Later, in the convent scene, Christ appeared among the nuns and joined them in a dance. Subsequent scenes took place in the "Bar of the Immaculate Conception" and, for the finale, a Nazi concentration camp.

Unsurprisingly, the singers were not able to perform their parts with conviction. This was a revival of a production dating from 1996 and, not having worked with the original director, Hans Neuenfels, they appeared not to have the slightest idea what they were supposed to be or to do. Like, I assume, most in the audience, I found the succession of confusing images on the stage completely mystifying. The synopsis of the opera in the programme did not help me, because it simply provided a conventional account of the plot of *Trovatore* and this bore little resemblance to what I had been watching.

After the synopsis, the programme contained a short piece by Neuenfels describing the slaughter of a bull, but with no indication of its relevance to *Il Trovatore* or to his interpretation of it. To be fair, there then followed some notes by the *Dramaturge* (the theatre's literary editor) on the preparation of the production. These at least offered some general, if not particularly insightful, observations—for example, "irrational forces dominate this opera"—and an occasional hint of what was the director was trying to achieve in various scenes. But, whether or not this was helpful, it is surely the primary responsibility of the director to communicate to the audience directly through what happens in the theatre, rather than requiring them to rely on explanatory notes in the programme.

The garish visual images of the Berlin *Trovatore* did not make one sympathetic to this production, but of course it was its complexity and incomprehensibility which constituted the biggest obstacle to appreciation. That complex productions may nevertheless be effective is borne out by the Bayreuth *Parsifal* which I described at the beginning of this chapter. Another example would be Christof Nel's 2005 staging of *Idomeneo* in Cologne. This work is, in content and spirit, the closest Mozart ever came to Greek drama. Set in the aftermath of the Trojan War, it is concerned with how destiny is determined by the consequences of agonising decisions which have to be made. In this case Idomeneo, the King of Crete, to be saved from a shipwreck, promises Neptune to sacrifice the first person he meets—it turns out to be his son Idamantes.

Nel chose as his setting a desolate place which could have been in post-Second World War Germany, but some of the costumes suggested also the contemporary Middle East—the performance took place at the time of the Iraq War. At the beginning, instead of there being a shipwreck, Idomeneo was, tortured by his head being pushed into a fish tank. Throughout the drama he appeared traumatised, as he tried to regain equilibrium and relate to the people, particularly his family, around him. And, at the end, it remained ambiguous whether order had been restored through his renunciation of power in favour of Idamantes.

Of course, the detailed action on the stage was far removed from the work's libretto, but the psychological interpretation offered was convincing, as aided by the austere visual images (designer Jens Kilian) which were compelling, if not always pleasing to the eye. The audience had to work hard to make sense of it all but if, like me, they found it ultimately very satisfying, I suspect that this was because the production served so well Mozart's brilliant, intense, and introspective score. Demanding musical theatre, yes, but also great musical theatre.

"Awful" is rather the epithet I would use to describe the performance of Handel's *Orlando* which I saw in Essen, also in 2005. Now, it may have been acceptable to treat the piece, which is the story of a soldier driven mad by unrequited love, as primarily a study of insanity, but the style of the production and its movements were incompatible with Handel's musical idiom. What Hytner had demonstrated with his *Xerxes* was that the old master's dependence on formal structure requires some visual equivalent, and the frantic, inconsequential scurrying around the stage of the crazed Orlando clashed with the rhythmic pulse of the score. So also the languorous beauty of the slower numbers in the score deserved something better than what was offered by director Tilman Knabe and his designer Alfred Peter: in the foreground an office, where Orlando is supposed to be employed, with a jumble of upturned tables and chairs; and, in the background, behind glass, a kitsch woodland in which he can jealously observe images of his girl's amorous saunterings.

When I encounter productions like this, I often wonder how it is that singers and conductors tolerate the perversities with which they have to be associated. And I am reminded of a striking scene in "The House", a TV documentary of 1996 made about the running of the Covent Garden Royal Opera House during the Jeremy Isaacs era. Nicholas Payne, Isaacs' lieutenant, was given the difficult task of persuading Bernard Haitink to conduct a production of the *Ring* for which he had an evident antipathy. Payne and a colleague tried to explain to Haitink the ideas behind Richard Jones' admittedly strange production. "Maybe I'm too old-fashioned," commented the famous conductor, "but if I can't understand it, I don't think that the audience will either." Yes, Maestro, a point well made.

You will have noticed that most of the productions described in this section, as well as the *Rienzi* and *Parsifal* with which I opened this chapter, were mounted in Germany. And, indeed, it is there that "*Regietheater*" (to be loosely translated as theatre dominated by the director's interpretation) has taken greatest hold. Radical departures from the original text and setting are commonplace. Although the intention may be to avoid the clichés of conventional, realistic productions, it is striking how many of the images regularly to be seen on the modern German stage have themselves become clichés: tables and chairs overturned; battered suitcases and empty beer cans on the floor; a decor of walls which are bare unless daubed with graffiti. Characters in whatever roles and of whatever gender scruffily dressed in slacks and open shirts. And anything attractive to the eye to be avoided at all costs.

Although *Regietheater* can be experienced in many parts of the opera world, there are differences. British and American audiences are more comfortable with realistic productions, whether or not updated, perhaps because the Anglo-Saxons have a mistrust of intellectual approaches and abstract ideas. In France and Italy, unusual interpretations are tolerated but aesthetic values are regarded as important and what appears on the stage must at least look good. So why has the deconstructionist approach, sometimes enlightening but often perverse and ugly, been so prevalent in Germany?

One possibility is that German audiences are more interested in, or at least tolerant of, the approach than their foreign counterparts. I doubt this: my experience suggests that they have been as irritated as I have been with some of the horrors perpetrated on them. On the other hand, although they often boo the production team at first nights, it would seem that this does not have much influence on artistic policy.

Money may be a major factor here. In the UK and USA, opera companies are extremely dependent on box office receipts and private sponsorship. This makes the company management wary of alienating the opera-going public. The productions at the New York Met have, for example, been notoriously conservative because that is what the private funders want, and they wield so much power there. The level of public subsidy of the performing arts in Germany is, in contrast, very high and this may, to some extent, insulate artistic policy against pressure from opera-goers. It is also the case that in many German towns taking out a subscription for the local opera company has traditionally been almost a civic responsibility, and therefore discontent would have a less obvious impact on the attendance statistics.

It is not always appreciated that the stage director is a relatively recent phenomenon in operatic history. Until the First World War, there was simply a "stage manager" who was responsible for arranging the singers' movements and the props. Even the limited role of that functionary could be the subject of adverse commentary, such as that of George Bernard Shaw, writing in 1891.

"As for prison doors that will not shut, and the ordinary door that will not open, I do not complain of that: it is the stage way of such apertures. One gets at last to quite look forward to Valentin [in *Faust*] attempting a dashing exit through an impracticable door in his house opposite the cathedral, and recoiling, flattened and taken back to disappear ignominiously through the solid wall ... I would not now accept any house as being that in which Rigoletto so jealously immured his daughter, unless the garden door were swinging invitingly open before every onset of the draughts, more numerous than the currents of the ocean, which ventilate the Covent Garden stage ... "

We have moved on a long way since that time. When, in 1967, Harold Rosenthal published his *Short History of Opera at Covent Garden*, he divided it up into "The Reign of the Singer, 1732–1903", "The Dictatorship of the Conductor, 1903–1939" and the "Age of the Producer, 1945–?". By "producer", Rosenthal meant of course what we now call the director, and the question mark was apposite because it is doubtful if he could have envisaged the extent to which directorial interpretation has become so important since 1967.

As the importance of the director and—we should not forget—also of the designer has grown, so have their capacity and desire to be inventive. This should not surprise us. Artists need to make a name for themselves, present their work in a distinctive way, stand out from others. Were, say, a *Figaro* or a *Rigoletto* to be staged just like hundreds of other productions in the past, the names of those responsible for the staging would hardly be noticed.

Ah yes, you might respond, but the same might be said of singers and conductors and no one would tolerate their approach to the music being as cavalier as that adopted by many directors to the libretto. True, but there are, I think, differences. It is the combination of music and drama in the original which speaks to us across the time period since its creation, not the particular way it was staged. Provided that the production is true to the spirit of that combination, liberties can surely be taken with it.

There is another aspect to this. Singers and conductors are part of an operatic performance and thus communicate directly with the audience; their artistic endeavours are in a real sense "live". Directors and designers, on the other hand, are involved only in the preparation of performances, and appear before the public, if at all, only on first nights. Psychologically that may encourage them to make greater efforts to "say something" and thereby make their mark.

Diversity in the staging is also important. There are about thirty core repertory operas which most companies will want to stage once every decade or so. Many opera-goers will see each of them three or four times, and maybe more. Will they want the same visual presentation of the work each time they return to it? I remain doubtful. As we know from Shakespeare, great drama lends itself to different interpretations and the same must apply to opera. Take *Cosi Fan Tutte*. This can be played, and enjoyed, as an entertaining comedy about infidelity but, as I pointed out in Chapter Seven, it can also be given as a serious and very moving piece about human jealousy. Neither approach is "right" or "wrong". And it is refreshing to come back to a piece and find in it new insights.

Diversity is nevertheless not to be confused with an insistence on novelty. It can, perhaps should, include what is orthodox or traditional. A young Belgian friend of mine became an enthusiastic opera-goer in 2003–4 and within a few years had seen, in Germany and the Netherlands, as well as in Belgium, many of the famous repertory works. He once complained to me that he had rarely encountered a traditional, realistic production. He was not hostile to modern interpretations, but rightly observed that novelty loses its power if you have had no experience o what is conventional, even old-fashioned.

I have been more fortunate. As this chapter reveals, my experiences of opera-going over a period of fifty years have enabled me to see a wide range of production styles, and the development of those styles has been exciting, if sometimes also disconcerting. I am certainly not nostalgic for the "good old days" when "what you saw was what the composer and librettist intended". Indeed, much of what I saw in the early days was, in dramatic terms, pathetically dull, offering little more than a staged framework for the singers and their music.

Opera is alive and kicking in the twenty-first century precisely because it has been rejuvenated. Of course there is a price to be paid for this and I am not talking about the exorbitant sums that are charged for tickets in the major international houses. When you attend modern, interpretative productions, you do not know whether you will emerge from the theatre in a state of euphoria, or rather fuming with rage. Those are the delights and disappointments of operatic experiences.

INDEX

ABOUT THE AUTHOR

Anthony Ogus is a retired academic lawyer. He was educated at St Dunstan's College, London, and Magdalen College, Oxford and is now Emeritus Professor at the Universities of Manchester and Rotterdam. He has written books and articles on the law. In 2002 he was awarded the CBE and in 2007 elected a Fellow of the British Academy.

Throughout his adult life, he has had a passionate interest in the arts. He has published reviews of concerts and opera performances. He gives talks on opera and music and is also a reader of audio books. He lives in Goldsborough, North Yorkshire.

Personal website http://www.anthonyogus.co.uk/